Hey Ladies!

Fourth of July, 1999

~~Dear Sharon~~,

I saw her on a talk show and found her to be hilarious. I hope your do too. Anyway, it's fun summer time reading. See you next month.

~~[crossed out signature]~~

Kennedy

Main Street Books

Doubleday

NeW YoRK

LOnDOn

ToRonTo

sYDneY

AuCKlanD

TALES

AND

TIPS

FOR

CURIOUS

Hey

GIRLS

Ladies!

A Main Street Book

PUBLISHED BY DOUBLEDAY
a division of Random House, Inc.
1540 Broadway, New York, New York 10036

MAIN STREET BOOKS, DOUBLEDAY, and the
portrayal of a building with a tree are trademarks
of Doubleday, a division of Random House, Inc.

Library of Congress Cataloging-in-Publication Data
Kennedy, 1972–
Hey ladies! : tales and tips for curious girls /
Kennedy.
p.   cm.
"Main Street books."
1. Teenage girls—United States—Life skills
guides—Juvenile literature.   2. Teenage girls—
United States—Conduct of life—Juvenile
literature.   I. Title.
HQ798.K45   1999   98-33357
646.7′00835′2—dc21   CIP
                                AC

ISBN 0-385-49094-1

Printed in the United States of America

First Main Street Books Edition: May 1999

1   3   5   7   9   10   8   6   4   2

BOOK DESIGN BY JENNIFER ANN DADDIO

For Ma

Contents

Hey Ladies!

HeY Ladies!

Hey Ladies! Thanks for picking up my book. I wrote it just for you. I hope you get as much from reading it as I did from writing it, but I think that's impossible because I lived a lot of what I wrote. Many of the ideas in here were born of situations I either overcame or completely messed up and would love to go back and change. If I had learned a lot sooner not to beat myself up for how my body looked, not to take my family for granted, not to worry about how I dressed, and basically to just enjoy being me I think I would have been a lot better off. Life basically boils down to experience and the choices you make and this book is about some of mine. It's about being yourself and having a great time doing it. It's about not compro-

My first MTV publicity shot, taken while I was in the midst of a massive pajama fetish.

mising and trying to experience things for the right reasons. It may sound corny if I say be nice to your grandmother and try to save some loot for later, but after surviving a sometimes rocky adolescence I wish I had done these things more often. Obviously nothing in here applies to everybody, but having the chance to share a lot of it has made me so happy. It has been such a challenge to narrow down what I want to say that I've touched on everything from the trivial to the absolutely essential, so take what you want and apply what you will. I hope you do so with a ton of character and the ease of knowing you've made your own choices for the right reasons. Enjoy! Love, Kennedy.

WhAT aBouT YoUr
Friends?

Without our friends we would be walking around alone. We would never play pickle ball, because who has time for pickle ball with strangers? We wouldn't have giddy discussions on the phone, it would be all telemarketers asking what kind of soda we drink and what brand of enema bag we use. Friends are pretty much everything, the squish in our organs, the crinkles in our smiling faces, the decadent fun in shared adventures and secret promises. If I didn't have my cement friends my building would have crumbled a long time ago. What is the point of doing anything unless you have people to share it with?

Friendship is a phenomenon that baffles scientists and psychologists alike. It is friendship that keeps old people happy and young people from aging too soon. Potentially you can be friendly to anyone, but what about the mysterious platonic connection that makes two people friends, allowing them to inhabit the same space and share the same jokes without strangling one another?

I have had the same best friend since I was eleven years old. Her name is KiKi and if you notice the many references to her it's because

3

we were physically inseparable from junior high until I left home and drove to California when I was eighteen. We talk all the time and she is still the one I rush home to call  when anything happens, even if it's three in the morning and I'm just bored. She's married now. Her husband Chris gets a little annoyed at this but we just give him our favorite saying from when we were kids: "Love is only chatter, friends are all that matter." KiKi and I used to work tirelessly to come up with inside jokes and phrases that we could use to secretly make fun of anyone or to annoy them so much that they would leave immediately. Amid all the deliberate jokes and punch lines we had an unspoken bond, the silent language that friends discover instantly and master as their lives evolve. KiKi and I have been through so much both together and separately, it is almost a miracle that we still speak and gossip as often as we do. The only thing I can imagine is that we were meant to be together. She and Chris are stuck with me.

It takes a lot to be a best friend. I don't think I could spend the energy on more than one person. You have to valiantly defend a friend's reputation by knocking down myths and lies or by changing the subject when someone brings up her name in an unpleasant light. You have to phone and write regularly if you're apart. You have to indulge the other's food

KiKi and me at our high school graduation in 1990.

4

cravings, you have to be on constant call for middle of the night pre-menstrual blubbering. You have to hold her hair back when she pukes, creatively assist her in getting ungrounded, agree that she is right whenever she fights, and always steer her in the right direction when things are taking a nasty turn. You basically have to be there in every way, always prepared to have fun at the drop of a hat or to indulge her aching heart with chocolate and vegemite when she's been left in the dust. Friends, especially *best* friends, never, *never* go for the same guy. If she liked him first, even if it's painfully obvious he likes you best, always let her have him. There will be plenty of men but there's only one of her. Assure her she looks great in everything, and on the off chance she doesn't kindly and gently suggest she try another shape and color. If you are lucky enough to have a very best friend, guard that friendship with your life because they're hard to come by and worth a lot of trouble. Nobody wants to end up playing pickle ball alone.

What About Your Friends?

DaNCiNg Queen

I don't think I'll ever forget our school cafeteria. Usually it was a high-carbohydrate, high-fat, skin-disrupting haven of Hostess Suzy Q's, co-agulated bean burritos, and corn dogs. Seasonally that mealtime romper room became a ballroom and a battlefield where, in the midst of temporary black light and a rented smoke machine, I fought for my self-esteem. Yes, I am talking about school dances. At my first few dances I was a disgrace, all flat chest and big eyes staring into the darkness, longing for a pubescent prince to drag me onto the floor for a five-minute grope during Madonna's "Crazy for You" (at the time the ultimate junior high mating anthem). Instead KiKi and I would hang out and laugh at ourselves because she had two fake front teeth and a back brace for her scoliosis, and me because . . . well, I was me. I soon realized the boys didn't want to grapple with a wallflower's training bra during the slow ditties. They would wait out the fast songs staring lust-fully at the good dancers, trying to think up the ultimate line to get those talented toe-tapping tamales into their clutches. Meanwhile, I was a total goofball during the quick numbers. Oh yeah, I could stick

7

my butt out, convulse distastefully, and run in circles, but it's safe to say that I could not cut a rug with an ounce of grace or agility. Then one day it happened. I was in a semicircle with a few of my pointy-shoed, headband-wearing chums when Colin the superstar athlete came up to us, looked at me mid-gyration, and blurted "Wow! You really can't dance!" Oh curses! The light of feminine shame shone from me so brightly it burned his ego and changed the course of my career in junior high school. I needed to learn how to dance. It was no longer an option, it was a matter of life and lonely limb.

I watched Molly Ringwald dance in her suburban white girl way in *The Breakfast Club,* the John Hughes mid-eighties classic about how a band of dissimilar teens bond one day in Saturday school. I studied the synchronicity of her wrists as they jutted out in perfect time to her fancy soccer kicks when she danced on the desk. I also watched Madonna (the mother of our Lourdes) countless times in "Like a Virgin" and later "Papa Don't Preach" (whoever thought Danny Aiello was Madonna's dad? Go figure!), demanding of myself the subtle perfection and timing she was blessed with during each three-minute mini-masterpiece. This one girl Ami actually *memorized* the entire dance from "Papa." Can you believe it? I still marvel at the dedication. I can't say I had the wherewithal to record all of those moves in the recesses of my young yet quickly maturing mind. Still, in long, self-indulgent sessions I reenacted in the mirror, verse by verse, step-by-step, each move that I would try to master (from what I understand this is a time-honored technique still used by the Laker Girls). When my brothers were off locked in the bathroom reading *Playboy* (the articles on motorcycles of course) and my parents were at social functions, I would slip in Depeche Mode and sashay in front of the full-length mirror in the hall. Oh the sweat! Oh the hours! Oh the embarrassment when my oldest brother walked in and cackled at the sight of me wearing spandex and a half T-shirt, immediately yelling for my other brother Al to come see what I was up to. They just walked away laughing with their sprained wrists and gave me the nickname I still can't shake. "Dick."

Time wore on, the moves in front of the mirror were coming a little slower than expected, and the Waluau (a clever amalgamation of our junior high school's name, Waluga, and the ever popular luau . . . what will they think of next?) was creeping up like a pair of panties during dodgeball. I was desperate, I was understocked in the motion department, I was a dancing spleen. My friend Hanna was having one of her fantastic sleepovers (did I mention she has four brothers?) and she and a few other ladies agreed to show me a thing or two in her living room. Armed with a copy of an album by Berlin ("riding on the Metro . . .") and wall-to-wall carpet, these sisters of mercy each took to a piece of furniture one by one and demonstrated their God-given abilities. They could do the Molly, the Madonna, even the Belinda Carlisle . . . the founder and *queen* of suburban boogie. It became a little embarrassing when they had to move my limbs for me in a desperate attempt to cure my arrhythmia. I felt like Gumby. A dorky, underdeveloped, short, stiff-legged white girl Gumby with a snowball's chance in Palm Desert of getting the attention of the hairless wonders I coveted on the Y chromosome side of the fence. But with practice, it came, slowly, tragically, eventually . . . it came. It was not in time with any music playing *out loud* but it was a start.

Our dances were held after school, never at night, so when the three o'clock bell rang I was ready for the dance. Fruit hat, capri pants, and aloha print shirt in hand, I was as determined as I was desperate to win the affection of anyone silly enough to return it. The lights dimmed, the music began, and I was off. Who knows what they played, I was too busy biting my lip in a concentrated frenzy as I tried to remember all the advice my friends gave me. The beats changed but I was too immersed in myself, looking down at my shoes, feigning coordination and dexterity, almost too busy to realize I was being watched. Not by that creep Colin, but by a boy who had realized sooner than I that "Crazy for You" had begun and it was time for a little preteen lovin'. I almost acknowledged his stare with some hideous loudmouth remark but stopped myself just in time to hear those priceless words: "Do you want to dance?" Instead of my stock flippant reply, "Yeah, numb nuts, what do you think I've been doing for the last half hour?" I sucked it up, looked into his eyes, and said, "Yes." Just as I was finally nailing all the rump-shakin' tactics I realized I had completely forgotten to seek any advice in the slow dancing department. What the hell do you do? It took a little while, but eventually I realized the sweetest part about all the work you put into dancing is that at some point you put the whole thing in cruise control and rock back and forth at a much slower rate in someone's arms. That is when it all feels the best and the battlefield becomes a sanctuary. When it works out it's one of the best feelings in the world. So what are you doing sitting around, numb nuts? Get up off your booty and dance!

10

tHe Chicken THeOry

Why were ski jump noses invented? How come it's so easy to become a blonde? Why do cheerleaders do the funky chicken? Have you ever been frustrated by the cute, perfect girl in school? The one with immaculately matched expensive outfits, a Colgate smile, no acne, no cellulite, and a sickeningly cheery disposition? Well, I am no cub reporter, but I have taken it upon myself to do some post–high school research on the cute girls who went to my school, solely for the benefit of my readers. I wish I could tell you about all of the uppidy cheerleaders and snot queens gone astray since their days of teen stardom and clear complexions. There was this one girl, I'll call her Chicken, who flaunted her wrist-sized waist and hefty chest all around school like a good little cat in heat. She loved making the less adequate girls feel bad, flirting with other people's boyfriends, wearing tight clothes, breathing. She was the girl who showed up after every holiday break with a wardrobe of new clothes that took her until late spring to show off entirely. She dated and dumped the cute guys, leaving them bitter and useless, she wore really expensive prom dresses and drove her

11

dad's Porsche, she played good tennis. She was a massive pain in my ass, but she was doomed.

I'll never forget how when sweet Chicken clucked off to college, the whole neighborhood was so curious to see how she'd "turn out," you know, being a debutante and all. I just wanted to see if she'd get blotchy skin from too much sun (she went to one of those fancy southern schools where you take a required course in sun overexposure). She certainly exceeded my expectations when she came home for Thanksgiving! Chicken herself looked like a plump butterball turkey. She was wrecked! Her butt was huge, her mood was sullen, her face was peeling and aged, her reputation was soiled and she was *still* stuck up! Whenever KiKi and I are having a bad day we call each other up and talk about how Chicken used to be so popular and loved, how she made out with our dates on prom night and how she looked perfect every morning at school while *our* eyes were thick with the concealer that couldn't hide our dark circles and bags. Then the conversation gets fun as we gab on about how she gained the freshman fifty in six weeks, how her skin looks like crap, and how no one, not even her *parents,* likes her anymore.

The Chicken scandal is fairly common in girls whose peak in life coincides with a time when most people are experiencing misery on a daily basis. Girls like Chicken tend to flaunt their premature vivaciousness in tight sweaters, micro-miniskirts, hair flips, and bad attitudes. It's hard to live with, but there is hope for the rest of us late bloomers. It has been systemathematically proven that girls who reach this level of perfection early have a very quick turnaround time into personal misery, cellulite, and even bankruptcy; it's called "The Chicken Theory." I have seen just about every cute prima ballerina, party girl, rich chick (whatever you call these mutants) plummet into obscurity and yuckiness in as short as eight weeks upon graduation from high school. Conversely, I have also witnessed the reverse phenomenon experienced by the rest of us, which is known as "Late Bloomers Renaissance," or just LBR for short (hey! those are the initials of my old boss!). LBR was documented as early as the sixteenth century in parts of France. If a girl is naturally kind, generous, witty, outgoing, mentally gifted, or athletic then the chances are she may be a little hard on the eyes during her "developmental" years. Scientists have proven late bloomers often reach a long-lasting, fulfilling peak that could take flight well into her adult life, hence the LBR. A young woman who is snotty, full-figured, flirtatious, bitchy, clear-skinned, and rich is as good as the algae on pond rocks the second she leaves for higher education. Sadly for girls like Chicken it becomes a humiliating test of will so distressing you *almost* feel sorry for them.

Next time Rachel Rally Girl flaunts her size four body, muscular abdomen, and perky self in front of you on her way to flirt with your guy, take a second to visualize her sixty pounds heavier with a face full of lines and a heart full of hurt. Chuckle under your breath and remember The Chicken Theory. It happens to the best of them. Cluck!

tHE FIrsT
Kissing Bandit

How many times has this happened to you? You and Lucky Man spend an evening together cavorting and feeding each other biscuits and Jell-O with your fingers. He compliments you on your coveralls and sticks his tongue in your hair. The moon is growing dim on the rim of the hill, the aligned planets sing to you as only planets can when they serenade a perfect moment in two young lovers' lives. He blows his nose, mumbles about allergies, and stares deep into your baby bluish contacts. He takes a firm grasp of your shoulders, licks his auburn lips, and leans in closer . . . closer. You can feel his breath for an eternal second on your own lips, you taste the caramel corn he ate at the fair, you see his teeth between his parted lips . . . and . . . finally your lips press together. They tingle in recognition, they buzz at the awaited acquaintance, they mash like two sleeping slugs, gurgling back and forth, wet hens pecking feverishly in a teenage quest for more . . . ahhhh, the first kiss.

And then, a week later, when you've attended the limited edition rerelease of *Hudson Hawk* with Stan the Other Man, you find yourself in the back of his Toyota. He brushes the back of your neck as you lean forward to change the radio. It's that nauseating Celine Dion number from *Titanic* and for a brief moment, despite his dark brown eyes and curly black hair, Stan has become a succulent Leonardo DiCaprio . . . luscious, male, horny. Since you are in a deserted country lane a block from your parents' house, and since it is summer, and you didn't really hear from Lucky, this handsome stranger seems good enough to be your husband someday, or at least . . . good enough for right now. Boldly you touch his stubble chin, your fingers intertwine, the night air becomes still as the willows recite poems just for you. You take a deep breath and the desperation between the two of you hurts, you'll simply die of starvation if your souls are not fed by this kiss . . . this lasting, memorable . . . first kiss.

Isn't that sweet? The feeling lit in your heart at the first meeting with a stranger's mouth? Love finding a home? Isn't that . . . unsanitary? First Kiss Addiction, or FKA as it's known in adolescent medicine, is a common and debilitating phenomenon. FKA can strike without warning and it can be harmful, sometimes fatal to new relationships. First kisses that are based on empty feelings are typically an overreaction to the pheromones produced by the recipients' adrenal glands. Endocrinologists have been studying the dating and kissing habits of young people for generations in an attempt to get a grasp on this fetish. It starts off with the first, first kiss. Usually the contact with the kissee after the initial date or interlude is cut off, with no real time to forge a bond or establish intimacy. Thus the kisser feels gypped and constantly searches for a new set of lips to zone in on. She is trying to fill a void left by her previous adventures, and modern habits allow for kissers to strike and leave with no further contact. For those who have

16

Kennedy

been hurt by the stinging nettles of love, first kisses are a way to make contact, get a rush of excitement, and get out of a situation before it develops into, oh goodness, a relationship. FKA's know first kisses are hardly possible when one is involved in the big "R."

I know, First Kiss Addiction sounds harmless, even tender, but it accounts for some scary statistics. Many of the radical tonsillectomies between the ages of thirteen and twenty are performed on First Kiss Addicts who are mistaken for allergy sufferers or people with poor immune systems. Untold numbers of people with Herpes Simplex I are the victims of FKA; they wear their reminders on their lips and live with the pain that is the still incurable cold sore. Mononucleosis, the Kissing Disease, could be appropriately renamed the First Kissers Disease. I'm sure there are a lot of sleepy cubs out there who would give up more than a few first kisses in exchange for their energy, spleens, tonsils, nonherpetic mouths, and untarnished reputations. They make excuses for their repeat illnesses—I chewed gum from Sally's mouth, I drank from someone else's pop, I gave mouth to mouth again today at the grocery store. Whatever the cause may be there are people out there who need help. There are ways to get over FKA . . . here's how.

Get to Know Your Victim: A lot of women say they would not have taken their chances and rolled the dice on the tongue suckers had they known more about them and their loathsome reputations. Chances are there is a lot lurking beneath a young Jedi's sterling exterior . . . a string of unhappy women, hepatitis, strep throat. Do a little research before you take the tonsil dive.

Picture Him with Bad Breath: Once you know you like him, I mean really like him, taking his undesirable odors will become a little easier. Spend some time with him, get to know his breath before you swap oral fluids. Bad breath can be a sign of tooth decay, stomach illness, or poor oral hygiene.

Learn to Have Friends: It is so much nicer to have more boy friends than boyfriends. It's a lot easier to look someone in the eye when you know you didn't contract influenza from last month's interlude in the back of his pickup.

Protect Your Reputation: A lot of girls think as long as they don't "put out" they are doing the world no harm by indulging in a few first kisses. Oh yeah? Tell that to Suzy, the seventeen-year-old who reluctantly gave up her tonsils on a Friday night because some young thug lured her with his beautiful eyes into yet another first kiss. She was labeled a slut at her school, just for using her wily tongue on half the wrestling team. Be careful. Don't let this happen to you. No wrestling team is worth spending two weeks on antibiotics for.

We all love the feeling of a first kiss, but those who suffer from FKA know the warm and yummy can diminish when the privilege is abused. It feels like a mouth full of spinach and cat piss when it's forced too soon, it can ruin a whole night, a perfect attendance record, a reputation. You can get the great feelings of first kissing by taking a warm bath or eating a pound and a half of gourmet chocolate, but even after too much chocolate you feel nauseous and bloated. Too many first kisses can do the same thing, add empty calories onto your soul and cause a series of volatile and costly infections, real and imagined. Next time you're about to kiss some sweet stranger for the first time make sure he's the kind of guy you'd want to share a first kiss with again and again. Your tonsils will thank you.

thE Fruits Of Love

They can classify us as they will, but who has the time to live by some-one else's image of our bodies when it is so often negative? I started to rethink the different classifications for the female body recently, and it made me feel better, at least it made me hungrier. I have heard of bodies being described as apples and pears, but the menagerie of fruit seemed somewhat incomplete. I thought there was more to this fruit-body connection than simply shape. As long as we are all fruity, and fruit is the best thing going in my book, then maybe each body type is as sweet as its counterpart in the produce section. Imagine this:

Apple: ☺ An apple-shaped girl is meant to be top-heavy and more slender as her shape goes down. Nice, broad shoulders, an ample bosom, and slim legs. She might be, as apples are, sweet or tantalizingly tart—she could be sweet as cobbler or sassy as Granny Smith. Any way you slice her she's got a good head on her shoulders and she's all-American.

Pear: 🍐 Pears are the opposite, slim rib cage and waist, but a powerful set of legs and a nice ghetto booty, something to be proud of in any culture. The thick tissue doesn't have to be fat, it can be all muscle, so a pear would be an ideal runner, cyclist, or skier. Have you ever seen Picabo Street's body? She is a pear poster child, all thighs and butt, yet without those curves she wouldn't have gone on to win a silver medal at the Olympic Games in Lillehammer and a gold in Nagano in downhill and GS ski racing. Pears are aggressive and positive, but not conceited . . . not enough room for conceit in a fruit with a small head.

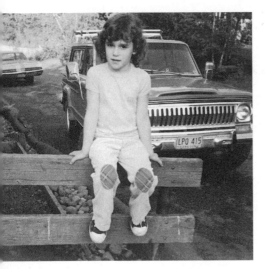

Me being a tough girl. Age six.

Banana: 🍌 As the commercial implies, perhaps the world's perfect food. Bananas are long and slender from head to toe and are sweet but not mushy. They are versatile without being overwhelming. If bananas are not ripe or mature yet they can be a little bitter and have a hard time making friends. Experience suits them well.

Watermelon: 🍉 A fruit that is beautifully colored. A watermelon is rotund, plump, and big. Watermelons are green with envy on the outside, but once they open up they are the greatest treasures. Watermelon girls are big from head to toe and are a whole lotta woman in every way. Small, malnourished watermelons have poor taste. They are much more pleasant when they are bigger and the most satisfying fruit friends once they accept themselves. It's a shame so many watermelons spend all their time trying to be bananas—they are so much more exotic and bright. We would all be better served seeing more of them in salads and in magazines.

Strawberry: 🍓 Itty, bitty, sweet as pie. Strawberry ladies are short and freckled, but very versatile in their many uses. They can be used in elegant dishes or steal the show in a down-home shortcake. They can run for class president or be a track star in the 1500 meter. The essence of a strawberry is sought after for candy and lip gloss because she is little, cute, and blushes easily. Even when cut down strawberries maintain their composure.

Pineapple: 🍍 These are unique fruits which are right at home in fun and warm climates. They are not quite as rotund as watermelons and they tend to have crazy hair which only elevates their enigmatic stature. When a pineapple is chill she lights up a room and sets people drooling. She doesn't like to have her clothes on and is never embarrassed by her size. She is a lovely compliment to any party, although she gets a bit wild when she drinks. She is loved by partyers and health freaks alike.

Kiwi: 🥝 These hairy little devils are quite seedy and green on the inside. They look odd but in the right context a kiwi girl sweetens the doldrums. Kiwis have a funny accent and taste best when they soften up. They are used to extensive travel and are well mannered even though they look like testicles.

Who doesn't love fruit salad? Whoever sits down for just a banana salad? Life would get so boring if we had only one fruit to chose from. Every single one tastes unique and wonderful in its own way, a compliment to any fruit bowl. Are our bodies any different? Just because you have pear legs and your best friend is a banana, does that make her any sweeter in a sophisticated torte? Heavens no! She would get all mushy and embarrass the guests. Boys are no different. They have to learn to love and sample the fruit platter, not just seek out the cute little strawberry because they saw her on *Party of Five*. There is plenty of room at this big brunch table of life for all the fruit, and there is plenty of room in the fruit bowl for all sorts of ladies. Instead of making the juices go sour by turning on one another we fruits have to protect each other from flies and freezer burn. There are a lot of pies to be a part of, a lot of plates to garnish. As long as we stay in it together we can reap the benefits into the sweet hereafter and share the room on the table with every variety.

i KnoW whY You'rE lOOkiNg aT
My Feet

I know the pain of short toes, since I have a shoeful of piggies that re-semble a radiation accident, or at least a really bad genetic joke. I see the girls walking around nowadays with their sweaters around their waists to cover their big bangin' booties, but that's a whole different chapter. I have weird feet that don't fit my body and that is my cross to bear (that is a catchall phrase where people liken their minuscule problems to anything Jesus suffered; it always makes me think of Alanis). I don't wear baggy clothes to hide anything, I wear big shoes.

It all started in my preteens, that impossible age where any sign of development is welcome yet painfully far away. Most girls wanted a training bra or tight jeans, I wanted toes that were a little longer. To this day when I feel the breeze lapping over the tops of my feet, or worse if I feel *my toes* exposed, I intuitively run inside for a pair of socks or some clogs. Yes, I will surrender all good fashion sense to cover the pigs in an emergency. I fortunately don't suffer from any foot ailments like nagging pain when I walk through the gardening depart-

25

ment at Sears. I leave that up to Grandma. But I can never seem to get the right vibe going for my feet in the summer and I *swear* part of the problem stems from wearing excruciating pointy-toed shoes all through junior high. The Doc Martens phase (remember grunge?) didn't start until the early nineties and I had graduated by then with a diploma, a strong dislike of the color beige, and a set of sad toes. The big one was way too big. What it lacked in length it made up in girth. The second toe nudged its way innocently enough atop the big one, sort of the way puppies do when they are done suckling off mom's teat and they just sort of crash on top of each other. The remaining three, what I like to call the "bench players," don't do much more than sit there and mope, never revealing any nail. And I surely don't paint my toes that often. Why waste the effort on one of the good Lord's practical jokes? My podiatrical life didn't have to turn out this way. If I had listened to my arches and toe knuckles screaming for mercy, if I had taken a closer look at the blood-soaked knee-highs and the milky blisters, I could have saved myself years of regret and longing and a good deal of cash at the cobbler's.

The point is—and there's always a point!—I would strongly advise you not to wear painful, pointy shoes for more than an hour and fifteen minutes a day. Go for something less deforming while your feet are growing. I hate to see anyone else live in a world of shy, pale feet complete with midget toes and a complex. I'm sure there are those "pain makes you beautiful" fascist leagues out there who really believe a woman hasn't lived until she's writhing in pain for the sake of beauty, but those are the masochists of the fashion world. Try the comfortable good-lookin' shoes for a change, not the impractical torture devices the stores and glossy ladies' magazines are pushing on you. Save the discomfort for a special occasion like the prom or a hot rod convention, and save yourself an outrageous plastic surgery bill rebuilding your golden arches. The pigs will oink with delight later in life, and that's some bacon we can all live with.

SoRRy, Ma

When I look back on my hotheaded days as a young rough do you know what I regret? Well, do you? Is it the last-minute attempts to get a passing grade in English or the nights I'd sneak out of friends' houses only to be chased around by hairy stoners, or is it the times I drank and smoked and stunted my growth and stained my teeth? No, those memories fade like tire marks in a snowstorm, only to be overshadowed by greater capers gone awry (although I do wish I had read a little more in high school). My one big regret, which I actually look back at and still wince about, are the harsh things I said to and the awful things I did to my mom.

My mom and me during my fifth-grade preppy phase.

Maria and I were so close all the way through sixth grade. I was proud to be like her and I loved to tell her everything. I painted pictures for her (she's an artist), I told her my dreams, I even slept in her

29

bed when I got scared. All of a sudden a rash of hormones and a distinct haughtiness overtook me like a masturbating trucker passing a Volkswagen on the way to a Kleenex factory. Instead of wanting to impress my mother I wanted to distance myself from her and do things to shock and disturb her. I wanted to be me, and me at the time was a self-centered, poorly balanced PMSing nightmare who stamped and fussed and played devil's advocate as often as a two-year-old plays peekaboo (I know a few two-year-olds, and trust me, peekaboo ain't goin' out of style). This deplorable tomfoolery (a distant relative of Chuck Woolery) had me in its grasp from the time I set my pink Gloria Vanderbilt–shod hoof into Waluga Junior High School until the day I walked across the stage at Lakeridge High School's class of 1990's commencement (do you know that commencement actually means beginning? Hmmm . . .).

My first act of terrorism on the Maternal One was sneaking out of the house at 2 A.M. on a Saturday night with five or six of my closest friends to litter the neighborhood with wads of toilet paper 📜 (oooh! dangerous liaisons). I soon progressed to weekend-long drinking binges disguised as "bonding weekends" at friends' houses when their parents were out of town. On one such occasion three of us decided to investigate the stimulating white trash activity known as "cruising." Cruising, for those of you not fortunate enough to live in a town where the next best thing to hanging out at the 7-Eleven is napping, is where a bunch of people drive around in a predetermined circle in embarrassingly pimped-out muscle cars 🏎️ (e.g., the '68 Charger or any Camaro) so the girls can get drunk and act slutty and the boys can try to talk them into doing it in a cornfield. The three of us set out in my friend Ann's mom's Buick to cruise a particularly unattractive section of SE

Portland armed with a six-pack of Budweiser and a drum of flavored lip gloss. The night was going smoothly until Little Annie made an illegal U-turn in front of a Portland police officer who was having a riveting night arresting young drunk cruisers. Ann tried to act dumb and say she lost her driver's license, figuring the cop would go "OK" and let her drive off into the night. Instead the cat found its way out of the bag and Ann's mom found her way into a cab to retrieve her presumably sleeping daughter and her malcontent amigos. Boy, was Maria in for a shock when she got that call to come get me at 4 A.M.! I recently asked my mom what went through her mind that night. She said, "Ya little twerp! I ought to break every bone in your body! No, just kidding. I was frightened. You ran into my arms and clutched onto me saying, 'I am so glad you are my mother' because one girl's mother was hitting her and you made me promise I would never hit you like that. A week later, don't you remember? A young girl got killed out on Eighty-second Avenue where you guys were cruising that night. That and passing out drunk at somebody's house were the worst things you ever did." When I asked her if she had trouble trusting me after that she said, "No, because I didn't think you would ever do anything that stupid again." What a mother. Fortunately she was right. I didn't go off the deep end, like so many lost lemmings can and do at some point. Instead I quit drinking a few months after that incident and have been a nondrinker for eleven years. I continued to throw tantrums and demand too much from my mom, but she was pretty understanding and weathered the storm. My mom went pretty easy on me through my teen years I think because I am the youngest of three and my two older brothers engaged in far more worrisome activity. I got to be the princess after all, and I got a car for my sixteenth birthday (nanny-nanny-nanny goats, boys).

taKe It EAsY on THe
Old Gal

Every mother-daughter combo is going to pave their relationship with sugar and salt, but you can make it easier on yourselves by following my simple plan.

Lay down your own law. Parents need to know where you are coming from and it will be easier to maintain control if you explain your position right off the bat. Have you heard the phrase "you can catch more flies with honey than you can with vinegar"? Well, truer words were never spoken, especially with Mom and Dad. Whenever you feel you are going to need space simply explain it *to* them instead of yelling *at* them. Instead of saying, "How dare you barge into my room without knocking! Can't I get any privacy?" you phrase it as "At this juncture in my life I am finding it necessary to create and maintain my individuality through extended periods of privacy and lengthy phone discussions with my peers so I can broaden my social skills and develop important leadership qualities. Thus, may I ask that you not disturb me when my bedroom door is shut? I promise we will have positive family

33

time later." You don't *have* to follow through on that last part, but the thought is beautiful and that's what counts.

Know how to handle an overheated discussion. When you have totally pushed past the acceptable margins of healthy daughtering and your mom responds with a battery of unladylike epithets, look her squarely in the eye and as calmly as possible say, "Are you done yet?" Boy, if this didn't help my mom calm herself and snap back to sanity immediately then I don't know what did.

Have a list. This is where your endless supply of energy and creativity comes in handy, especially on those late nights when you'd be cheating yourself out of life's precious moments by heading home too soon. When you are caught coming home at an unreasonable hour your adrenaline is working overtime, especially if you've crashed the car or have a visible hickey. It is crucial that you have a list of Teflon excuses in your arsenal to ramble off before the parent has a chance to speak, scold, or ground. It is best to run these little nuggets past your friends for refining and combining; having two or three at a time is powerful. Excuses are like those long-lost Garanimals . . . they work better combined!

"Sorry!" This is a magic word. Every parent wants to believe their daughter is an angel, and when you flash the puppy dogs after you know what you did was wrong and utter that five-letter word your mom will not only forgive you, but she will probably extend your curfew because she knows it is *you* she can really trust.

34

Live fast, think faster. Your brain will keep you out of most snafus in life so be sure to pack it with you when you travel, and don't impair your most precious organ (you know what I mean). The best advice I can give you transcends the parent-adolescent tree and applies to the whole forest. Don't do anything you will have to say you are sorry for. Don't knowingly screw someone over or talk behind their back or whatever the current temptation is when you know it is absolutely wrong. Your brain and heart, when operating in sync, will usually let you know when something doesn't feel right ahead of time. Obviously this step is impossible at times, but it will keep you out of a lot of fights with your parents and other dilemmas that pop up during this little obstacle course. My friend Crayton taught me this after I unfairly belittled him our senior year, and I think it hit home as much as any discussion I had in high school. If you don't do the wrong thing or say anything too hurtful in the first place you'll never have to say you're sorry and you'll never have to make excuses.

REbeL wIThOUt
a Clue

Manot is a fifteen-year-old friend of mine who is headed for the big house or the maternity ward at breakneck speed. A lovely, moon-faced child of brilliant liberal parents, Manot decided at a young age that it was more productive to be a naughty slacker than to participate in adolescence. Her drug of choice is marijuana, and her beau is a twenty-year-old LSD dealer in prison who gets weekends free to hang with her at her parents' home. A mother's dream come true! Her childhood was a storybook one that I envied when it was revealed to me by her dad, my good friend John. He loved to ramble about her stint with a prominent ballet company in New York when she was eight, and her ranking as one of the best swimmers in the state by her eleventh birthday. As he put it, anything she put her strong mind to she could master so effortlessly it even made him jealous, and he's a determined overachiever in his own right.

When I first met Manot she was an eleven-year-old little girl with big eyes and a chubby frame whose shoulders were constantly hunched over trying to conceal an awkward stage. All she talked about was how she wanted to be a model. A model! "How vapid" I often thought. I think all she really wanted was to feel like a pretty model. I don't think she was eager to go on three-week cocaine binges in Italy weighing twelve pounds. I knew in order to fully understand this developing diva I would have to speak to her honestly and find out why being bad feels so good.

Can I call you Manot in my book? No, it wouldn't be appropriate. I changed my name to Chloe. **Can I call you Chloe?** Yes. **How is your life?** Fast. I can't live my life slow. Some people have to move at a faster pace. It takes a certain kind of person to go to the limit. Instant gratification is a good thing. **Do you have an addictive personality?** Yeah, slightly. **Do you do drugs?** Yep. (Pause.) I don't do heroin or cocaine or crack or methamphetamines, but I do everything else. **Do you ever worry about getting busted?** Yeah, it's always a concern, but there are so many things people are doing that you have no clue about who don't get busted. The risk is there every time you go out. **How do your parents feel about this? Are you through being parented?** Yes. I spend so much of my time by myself I might as well do the whole thing by myself. It's not like I'm angry at my parents, although they did not make the right decisions when we lived in New York. They never let me model or get into acting. I could have had a serious career. I've always wanted to be famous since I was a kid and I knew what fame was. Not a lot of people were around when I was a kid, and all the important ones left, I guess, if you want to be psychological about it. When you are famous people look up to you and adore you. You have an impact on the world. I would like to be amazing and wonderful. I'd like to be glamorous. **Where do you see your life going?** I'm not sure. I might move to Arizona. I've been thinking about getting a house there with my boyfriend. **(Sounding like a mother.) How are you going to live at fifteen with no education and no money?** There are a lot of ways to make money. You can sell fruit or make clothes. **Which would you most likely do, sell fruit, make clothes, or sell drugs?** Sell drugs. Oh, and make clothes. For a couple years, not long-term. **Do you fear any physical repercussions from your drug use?** No, not negative. It's all been positive. I feel my perception growing. I can see and hear everything in every direction. I wouldn't say it won't have any effect, but the way I feel sometimes the repercussions are balanced out because I feel so good. I also love the feeling I get when people come up to me (at raves) and tell me they are having the most incredible feeling of their lives because of some Ecstasy I sold them. They feel great and can dance forever in front of thousands of people all night long. I love it. **What is your responsibility in society?** I don't have one. I don't fit into their classifications, their brainwashing. Being nomadic is better than work or school or the whole Mom-Pop-Sis thing. It doesn't pay off. **What happens if you get pregnant or go to prison?** Well . . . if . . . hmmm. That is a hard question. I guess I would call my friends and my other family. They would not look down on me if I landed in prison and with my friends prison is a very real thing. It is something I worry about, but I take precautions and use protection so hopefully that won't happen. **Do you have good self-discipline?** No. I have a good mind.

God. That conversation was depressing. You hear about girls with low self-esteem who come from broken homes and abusive families who live these seedy, seemingly fictional lives. Why does a suburban former ballerina and athlete turn into a drugged-out, Arizona-bound mess? It doesn't make sense. After talking to little Manot all I could do was cry over a cup of mint tea ☕ and imagine the horror that her mother must live through each day wondering where her daughter is, where she is sleeping, what she is on. I think that and I thank God I didn't take the wrong turn when I was that age. At fifteen you have the world figured out and you carry it around on a string. Unfortunately for Manot she got too carried away in her pursuit of the glamorous life and it looks like she's got just enough string to hang herself. Maybe being a model ain't such a bad thing after all.

iNTo THe Drink

If this book is an exercise in sharing some of what I've been given and some of what I've taken from growing up, then this chapter serves a crucial and serious function, because it's about a truly life-changing decision. What I most admire in people is the freedom and the trust shared by those who allow each other to live freely and take responsibility for their own actions. This is a philosophy I take on politically and something I strive for in my daily life, so when you read this chapter please bear this in mind: I am not trying to change you or preach to you, I just want to tell you how I came to my own conclusion about something very important. I could have gone the other way.

Getting drunk to me is an exercise in futility. It is expensive, it makes you smell bad, it tastes like cough syrup, and it is accountable for too many people losing control of themselves and consequently having the most precious things taken from them through rape, accidents, and overdoses. All this begins with the person who chooses to drink. I don't think you can blame the ills of alcohol on society or any particular group. However, a parent trying to force their kid into *not* drinking is like trying to coax vomit back into the stomach after it's left the esophagus. I know one of the biggest worries that keeps parents up late at night (other than fluctuating interest rates) is the thought of their baby losing it to alcohol or drugs. Unfortunately for them, the decision is not your parents', it is yours.

I chose to stop drinking at fourteen when I was so caught up in doing things for other people (not the right kind of things for others like working at a soup kitchen or taking better care of Grandma) that I didn't realize I despised the things everyone was glamorizing. I would drink on the weekends with my older friends. Twice during junior high I actually got drunk with two football players at school because I thought they were hot and would like me better if I drank. They were hot and they liked me better to my face, but when I turned around they called me names, in between calling plays in a huddle, I assume. For a spell two of my friends and I walked around and sold singing telegrams for a dollar each to raise money for wine coolers (hello, eighties?) to drink at this girl's party. You think I'm a card now, you should have seen all seventy-five pounds of me at that party trying to drink my own volume in wine and Jack Daniel's. I was a riot. Ha! How funny it must have been to watch me puke blood on my friend's white carpet. What a scream it was hosing me off outside on the porch as fifteen seventh graders sat around in tears. I would love to have been there, but I had passed out three hours earlier. And I bet I was the life of the party in the emergency room where they pumped my stomach. And hey . . . someone stole my jewelry. That episode should have been the catalyst for my sobriety, but it wasn't. It took two more years of people pleasing and self-abuse to realize that drinking and I were not compañeros (I heard that word in *Evita)*. By the time I decided to quit I was fourteen and had a pretty regular schedule going of beer and Mary Jane, pot, smoke, grass . . . you know, the wacky tobacky? I started getting really sick with kidney infections and strep throat, I was having fainting spells, and my periods were off. The doctor used to joke that he liked seeing me so much because it ensured his kids were going to get a great college education. I had a heart murmur, I was losing weight, I was pale, I was also a hypochondriac, for God's sake! It was after about five months of thrice weekly MD visits that the doctor sat me down and asked me frankly about my imbibing. Scared and sweaty, I told him the truth. I was a pretty regular drinker, I never blacked out and didn't do it during the week, I seasoned my drinking with a dash of marijuana, and I'd been doing so since I was ten. He listened intently, hardly shocked or emotional. He let me go on for a little while, and then he stopped me. He asked me in a hushed voice to stop drinking, to stop smoking, and to not even think about any stimulants for fear they would stop my heart. He was compassionate about what my family had been through since my parents' divorce and explained it was ludicrous for me to treat my body the way I was, to continue making it suffer all in the name of gaining attention and approval. Was drinking the best way to spend my time? Wouldn't it be better spent healing myself and making better decisions that would ensure my well-being instead of destroying it? For the first time someone had really left a decision like that up to me; it wasn't an adult talking down to me and telling me "no," it was a professional who presented me with all the facts and in a grown-up voice left the decision up to me. It was then that I chose to stop drinking, and I've happily been a nondrinker ever since. I don't consider myself "sober" and I don't attend meetings, but I do find that not drinking gives me a better perspective and allows me to feel a little more in control and very thankful, especially when I see my friends puking and complaining of hangovers and blackouts. I have had plenty of opportunities to drink and do drugs with all sorts of people, but I decided to take the opportunity to people-watch instead, to drink ginger ale, and to laugh at the girls who cry in drunken hysteria because their no-good-cheatin' man is kissing another barfly.

The decision is ultimately yours. It is so exciting to go to parties and meet new people and flirt with them across the room, to laugh too loud and share inside jokes with your friends, but maybe the decision you make will be to do all these things without alcohol in your system. Maybe you'll be the girl who holds everyone else's hair back when they puke, the one who takes Sprite to parties and gives everyone a ride home. Maybe you'll be the girl who gets to hear everyone's incoherent stories about how Mike the bastard left her at the party or how Ed the creep tried to take off her skirt, how the room won't stop spinning and . . . well, come to think of it, those stories could drive *anyone* to drink. Be one of the ladies who makes up her own mind, who does things to feel better, not just to be liked. And if you do drink? 🍷 Be responsible. Don't get so drunk you don't have the good sense to avoid getting locked in a room with a bunch of illiterate party boys whose favorite game is burst the hymen on the drunk girl. It happens . . . don't let it happen to you. Please?

Kennedy

mY fiRSt Kiss

I will never forget the night. It was shortly after a young politician named Randy had asked me to "go out" with him at a September school dance toward the end of a slow song. We had slow-danced twice, flirted in the hallway, his friend had asked about me—it was the first time a cute boy had shown any interest in me. A few months prior I had transferred from a very small school where all the boys and girls called themselves an item one week only to break up the next Tuesday. It was very casual. At this new and bigger junior high there was a bit more formality in dating and everyone seemed to know and adhere to the rules. I was a little clueless at first, having come from a communal microcosm, so I casually dated two other boys within my first month there and developed a bit of a reputation because, following the standards of the old corral, I broke up with them a week later when I got bored. My rep was only slightly tarnished at that point, though, so Randy felt comfortable in making my acquaintance and making me his girlfriend. As we danced that day, he whispered in my ear, "Will you go out with me?" and I accepted with a blush. I had to try and keep my cool, being a slut and all. The next night at a football game we walked around the track holding hands (like all the other junior high couples), picked out china patterns and a place for the reception, and ate Red Vines. I was a pert Easter egg all aglow with new love and security, I was ready to be kissed and taken to a magical, romantic place like Fiji. That place was my first boy-girl party the next weekend at my friend Toady's house. Toady is still my buddy. He's a funny redhead and I swear he wore makeup when he was sixteen. He said it was Oxy. Toady is one of those guys who experienced this great epiphany after college and really grew into his own amazing personality. During high school he was a little affected, so we drifted apart and didn't get to be friends again until he was almost done with his degree. That's when I realized he had metamorphosed back into a human. You will find that this happens with a lot of your guy friends during adolescence. I realize this is a huge digression from my first kiss, but it can be so disheartening when the guys you grew up with blossom into total jerks in the course of a few short years. They are your best friends one day, giving you advice and laughing at your jokes, and the next they are making fun of you in front of their friends, saying you have a big butt and ignoring you completely the rest of the time. They'll eventually get over it and in the end you have license to make fun of the painful insecurities they did such a poor job of masking in their evil years. Girls are a lot smarter. Anyhoo . . . back to me and Randy.

It was a Saturday and my mom dropped me off at Toady's party for some harmless, supervised dancing and some unsupervised lovin' if we were lucky (wink, wink). A few of us were in Toady's bedroom when he started going "C'mon, you guys, start kissing!" He could be such a dork! Randy was way above that chumpery, so he shrugged

Toady off and asked if I wanted to go outside. Gulp, tight throat, nervous skinny girl, don't screw it up. "Sure." It's always best to play nonchalant girl when you are about to get a smooch. He took my hand and we crept around the house without talking. He stood next to a fence that was hidden from the rest of the house, put his hands on my hips, and pulled me a little closer. He had so much experience! A woman knows these things, don't you think? I have low blood pressure. The moon was bright in the autumn sky and his little pink lips looked sweet and fresh. It was a little cold. I was still quiet (for once)

My eighth-grade graduation date, Rob. Some of the parents were "disgusted" by my dress. He didn't kiss me.

because I didn't want to say something wrong and kill the moment. I was ready. My stomach felt like I was on a ride at Magic Mountain where the bottom drops out and you free-fall for a few seconds that frighten you and amuse you all at once. He was smiling a happy little puppy smile and finally moved his face in close to mine and slowly planted a kiss that only the vice president of the student body would know how to give. It was all so yummy, like cookie dough and presents and tap shoes, it was something I had thought about so much and built up and feared. What are you supposed to do during your first kiss? How much are you supposed to do on the first night you become physical? What is he going to expect from me? He didn't maul me, he didn't rip off my Guess? jeans with the little ankle zippers. He just held my face, we pressed our lips together and became cotton candy for a few seconds that night. It was one of those nights you go back to in your mind when the mental computer is trying to pull up those fresh, sweet images to revitalize something tired inside.

Randy and I broke up a few weeks later. He called me up on a Sunday night and chatted with me for about twenty minutes about sports and school politics. Apparently his numbers were down in a straw poll and he needed to refresh his youthful image. Unfortunately I was not the refreshment. I got the ax. He broke up with me after wasting twenty minutes of my time pretending to still be my sweet junior high boyfriend with the cute puppy lips and the sugary hand-holding. He was the model for the next ten years of my dating future and he was ruining it by stringing me along with Sunday night small talk. That was the last time I dated someone in public office. The pressure to maintain a perfect relationship was too much, the facade too demanding. It was probably best we broke up when we did, you know, before we had children. I admit, it was hard for me to look Randy in the eye after that pride-crushing blow. It's hard to have your first love dump you on the side of the road like a sack of old hangers. It's OK now, the wounds have healed. He went on to date a bunch of perky rally girls and eventually became a religious fanatic in New Zealand (a beautiful country, you should see all the sheep!) and moves around the world with his group preaching their message of love and acceptance. Where was my love, Randy? Why couldn't you accept me? Was I a little too "fast" for you? Oh well . . . I was the girl who got the kiss in the moonlight at the boy-girl party. I got to be Mr. Vice President's junior high girlfriend for three weeks, and that suited me just fine. Your first kiss is hopefully the sweetest, and that goes hand in hand with first love, which is powerful and so untouchable in its emotion because your heart is so fresh and unscathed, so ready to fall so deeply in love, and it breaks so hard when it falls too fast. If you are too careful with your heart you will never fall completely in love and you won't experience the best part of life. Whoever your Randy is I hope he treats you well and basks in your sunshine. Just don't follow him to New Zealand. It's best to break up with someone before you become one of the sheep, no matter how well they kiss.

Zits

Oh you gotta love these devils! There isn't a picture in existence of me without some pus-filled red mound on the most conspicuous part of my face. No matter what I did to try and control my breakouts (gels, pads, tinctures, tonics, acids, masks, peels, scrubs, enemas . . . etc. . . . .) I always lost my *self*-control when I got in front of a mirror. There was a magnetic force that drew my fingertips right to the head of each crimson bastard and like a maniac I would pop, torture, and maim my own face. Every freakin' time I touched my face it always looked worse after a few minutes in front of the mirror. I had a useless strategy and everything! I'd get in this crazy stance with my knees slightly bent, shoulder width apart, resting against the sink so it could support my body weight enough for me to get close to the mirror without fogging it up. Then I'd stare at my reflection, eyes fixed on the devil mound, say, on my chin. I'd shake my wrists out (gotta be limber), flex my fingers, and go to work. First I'd push from the outside in, and if it were ripe enough you could actually begin labor . . . the tiny white head of the kernel popping out. What a tease! I'd do this pretty hard and just long

51

enough to make it bleed. I'd pat the blood off with a piece of wadded tissue, and thinking back to CPR I'd start applying direct pressure. At this point if the whole ball of wax (eewww!) didn't pop out logic and past experience would dictate it was time to put down the witch hazel and tissue, straighten my knees, and walk away . . . but no! This is when I would apply the death grip! I would try and *pull* the surrounding skin apart and force the insubordinate weasel from its niche. It had to give at some point! Yeah, it gave . . . it gave me a few good scars! There are two gems right next to each other on my forehead that look like I've been stapled. So I'd pull and curse and fog up the mirror until *finally* I'd walk away not because I was trying to save my skin, but because my fingers were too bloody and exhausted. It was like looking at a car accident on the highway. I was getting a stomachache! I never mastered the art of the pop, I still suck at it, and every time I come out of the bathroom with a newly formed scab or nail marks on my forehead my boyfriend laughs hysterically because he's seen the process up close. I've marred his face on more than one occasion (sorry!).

It wasn't until I moved to NYC that I *really* started getting bad breakouts. I thought I was over my hormonal fluctuations when I reached twenty, but really the fun had just begun (at least I didn't have backne). When I started my job at Televised Musicals they had me wearing this really thick waxy makeup that gave me a rash of zits that looked like hives. One girl suggested I try dissolving a powdered laxative in hot water and steaming the crap out of my face (no pun intended, I think). It eventually got so bad friends would call up and instead of asking how I was they'd start off with "You still fighting that losing battle against your acne?" I had to start seeing the dermatologist. She explained what was going wrong with my face: the adjustment to air pollution, too many oils in my hair and facial products, and I wasn't drinking enough water. She prescribed some topical antibiotic cream that I think was called benzomycin (a combination of benzoyl peroxide and erythromycin) that zapped my red nazi chin-invaders so well I bought the company! No, not really. Luckily, my problems were pretty easy to solve and really common. My skin isn't perfect now, but at least people have stopped staring and asking me how I survived the bee stings.

Another breakthrough I had in the skin department was life-saving and inexpensive. I was doing a fashion show in Paris (it was a fluke, I was really fat compared to the other girls, but it made me laugh because I could actually eat the cheese and butter baguettes without running to the bathroom to make myself puke) where this makeup artist Lucille gave me a lesson in sitting still and keeping my face for-ward. She was a little impatient at my stargazing at the other "real" models. See, models are really paranoid about the way they look, so Lucille took notice of the bumps on my face and decided to give me a piece of advice. She said in her cute French accent, "Do you know what I like to do when I am eating cereal in the morning that gives me really clear skin?" and I thought silently, "I don't know, have sex with your husband?" but instead answered aloud, "No, Lucille. What could you possibly do in the morning while you're eating your cereal that makes your skin smooth?" "Well," she said, in cute franglais, "I like put on my face mixing aff (French for *half)* cottage cheese, aff unny (translation: *half honey)* for ten minutes while I eat granola. It makes my skin divine." And this woman wasn't whistling french fries either, her skin was beautiful! If she weren't 5´ 2˝ with a really big nose and if she weren't thirty-five or so she could have been a model. Her skin was delicious! So when I got back from Paris (they don't have cottage cheese *anywhere* there! I hope I understood her correctly) I started mixing honey and curds together every day for about a week. I skipped the granola because I find it to be too precious to eat in the morning. I prefer Crunch Berries. I found if you use too much honey and runny curds the whole business sort of runs off your face, so drain the cottage juice a little before you apply it. I was amazed at how well this works. My skin actually looked nice for a change, especially after a week of eating Parisian dessert cheese and chocolate crepes every day. So, may I suggest for those with skin issues and a tight budget, buy some cottage cheese and honey, mix equal parts together, and put a nice medium coating on your face each morning for a week. If it burns try using it every other day (I'm sort of making these directions up as I go along, so bear with me). Once you see some nice results you can taper down and use it only every few days. If it works, great! When *you* do a fashion show in Paris and Lucille is your makeup artist be sure to thank her for both of us. If it doesn't work then don't do it anymore, but don't blame me, I didn't make it up. Not every remedy works for everyone, but this one is cheap and easy, so there you go. I hope your skin is smooth and milky and your zits form only at night just to disappear in the morning.

Kennedy

a DErMatOIoGIst
Pores Her Heart Out

Dr. Ellen Gendler is one of those New York dermatologists who is concerned and vociferous. The stars flock to her and the magazines will halt the presses for a quote. She took time out from her lecturing, poking, and squeezing to enlighten me about zits, skin care, and sunscreen. She's a nice lady.

What is your specialty? General and cosmetic dermatology. **What is a zit?** Oy! A zit is an inflamed spot that occurs around an oil gland and generally is a reaction to a combination of oil plus bacteria from the hair follicle and oil gland. **Why do we get them?** Some people blame stress for pimples but there has never been any direct link. Diet is generally not believed to have any impact on pimples at all. There are many causes, like heredity and hormonal abnormalities, and sometimes medications can do it. **What can you do to stop a breakout before it starts?** If you are someone who is prone to breaking out you need to use medications on a regular basis. You can't just expect to put some topical medicine on a pimple and have it disappear by the morning. **Do those pore strips work?** No, not really. In fact, they can be very irritating and can actually pull the skin off your nose if you are not careful. The strips stick to the skin and they really need to be wet to be removed easily. But very often, teenagers who are kind of overzealous in their application or who leave them on too long, end up having them literally rip their skin. I never recommend them. **Can you overwash your skin?** Sure. **Can you get zits from dry skin?** No. You can break out from too much moisture. **What can you do if you discover a zit the night of a dance or a function?** Well, if you are near your dermatologist's office you can go in and have an anti-inflammatory injection. That is probably your best option. Otherwise you can't really do a lot except cover it up. **What is the best way to pop a zit?** Oy! These are tough questions, because I really don't encourage any laypeople to pop their own pimples. Even when they attempt to sterilize a needle, by holding it over a flame, sometimes they will get little pieces of carbon at the end of the needle and then end up depositing carbon under their skin. So, I recommend that they leave it alone. **Really? I have done that. I have burned a needle or a pin thinking, "Oh, I've just destroyed the bacteria." But the black stuff at the end can get into the** . . . Sure, and then you have a little tattoo. **Should an adolescent girl be getting facials?** No. **Why not?** I don't think anybody should really get facials unless they have a lot of blackheads that can be extracted. **What do you think of alphahydroxy products for young skin?** It depends on the skin. If they are not too irritating, I think they are fine. But the most important thing is that the adolescents start using broad-spectrum sunscreen to prevent sun damage. **What is the most common skin care mistake girls make?** I would say picking at their pimples or using too much moisturizer. **What can you do for puffy, tired eyes?** Sleep on an extra pillow. It

56

helps keeps the fluid from pooling under the eyes and making them look puffy. **Do carbonated beverages and salt make your eyes puffy?** Well, salt can make you retain water and then if you have any loose skin under your eyes that would be a place that it would be reflected. **What is the worst thing for your skin?** The sun is probably the worst thing for the skin, although cigarettes are a close second and the combination of sun and cigarettes is really horrible. **With all the anti-wrinkle agents on the market, isn't it safe to say I can destroy my skin and repair it later?** No. Totally not. **Why not?** Because these products don't completely repair the skin. They may help reverse some of the damage, but they can't repair all of it. It is like saying you'll quit smoking and reverse all the damage you've done to your lungs. It is just not possible. **Why is it important to take care of your skin?** Your skin is your largest organ and certainly your most prominent one. It is the first thing people see when they look at you. **What overall beneficial program can you do for your skin that would give you a glowing and acne-free appearance?** Well, glowing and acne-free don't necessarily have anything to do with one another, but I really think the most important thing for the long haul is to stay out of the sun. Because that will ensure that as you get older you will have the best-looking skin possible. I would say stay out of the sun by using a broad-spectrum UVA and UVB sunscreen. Choose one that contains something called avobenzone (also known as parsol 1789), which blocks UVA rays and really helps minimize damage from the sun. That is the most important thing. Also avoid overusing moisturizers so that you don't get clogging of the pores, which can eventually cause permanent dilation of the pores. And avoid smoking at an early age so you don't get hooked on it and deprive your skin of oxygen as smoking does. **What is the lowest daily SPF that you would recommend?** 15 **Who is at** most risk for skin cancer? Fair-skinned, light-eyed people. **What is the safest way to get a tan?** Not to. **Are tanning beds safer?** No! They are not safer at all; in fact, they are probably less safe because they are concentrated UVA rays which penetrate deeper into the skin and probably in the long run cause more damage to the skin than the UVB rays. **When does the worst sun damage occur? What time of day?** The strongest rays of the sun are usually between the hours of 10 A.M. and 3 P.M. That is when you would have the greatest chance of getting a burn. **At what age are you most vulnerable to long-term sun damage if you get a sunburn?** Forever. If you burn when you're young, well, obviously it shows up when you are an adult. If you get a terrible sunburn when you are forty you have a chance of it showing up when you are sixty. **Is there anything else that you want girls to know?** The only other thing that I would caution them against is doing a lot of steaming to their faces because that causes the blood vessels to dilate. **Yeah. Steaming is very popular. There are a lot of myths out there that say facials are just the end-all.** Those are myths. Dumb! **Dr. Gendler says, "Facials are dumb."** Well, you don't have to say that, but especially when they are done by people who are not experienced, who pick and squeeze and do more destruction than anything else. **Except for smoking in the sun without sunscreen while wearing too much moisturizer with light hair and eyes.**

Kennedy

Party

aLL tHe TIme

No matter your age, parties can be one of the most anxiety-ridden events in all of human existence. Crowded rooms, unknown faces, noise, smoke, music  . . . the greatest and worst moments take

place at parties. At every stage of your life you will probably have to make some kind of statement at a soiree. Whether it's a family tree-trimming or an all-out parentally unsupervised extravaganza, you'll either have to make a stunning entrance or wear something divine. My first *big* and angst-riddled party was my freshman year in high school, where all the big football players were shotgunning beers, cool kids were smoking on the porch, and cou-

Me and the boys hanging out at our high school graduation party.

ples were pawing one another on the couch. Do drunk people know how funny they look when they make out all sloppily in public? Even today in bars I see a guy and a girl kissing in their unfamiliar, drool-puddled glory and I laugh so hard thinking of their nasty breath and the next day's regrets. "What was I thinking?" she'll ask her friends, mortified. "Dude, did I score?" he'll inquire of his friends as they try to sort through the blackness and fog of the previous night. But anyway, I love parties. They are so scary, so dramatic, a time to escape and look your best while trying to play a nonchalant role. You *try* to act as naturally as you can while you're dressed up to the gills. The worst party is when you are alone and seeking desperately for a familiar face or a new friend and all you get in return is a bunch of cold faces staring you down. The best party is when you laugh so loud you nearly vomit and jump around and scream with your friends, when you feel like you own the place and have license to do whatever you want, like you're immortal (if you can go through your entire youth with that feeling you'll be better served the rest of your life). You can have that great feeling every party you go to . . . no, seriously! Do you realize what you give off to other people when you walk around with your shoulders hunched, avoiding eye contact and cowering around like a naked Chihuahua? Can't you see what message you are sending? Instead of cowering try these little things next time you venture into the swamp of Friday night righteousness.

Act Like It's Your Party: This is the best advice for party-going, especially if you are in over your head and don't know anyone. Instead of avoiding the stares of the men and the ladies in the house pretend they are *your* guests and were honored to have you invite them. People will actually pick up on your confidence and will think you are vibing them. I went to a big fancy schmancy Hollywood party with my friend Stephen and I didn't know a soul! He was off schmoozing with Andie MacDowell and Winona Ryder while I was left trolling for dip with my head down at the buffet. Instead of finding a nice quiet study and watching CNN all night (my natural inclination when I'm uncomfortable), I padded around the joint like I owned the place and waved hello to people from across the room. It's the absolute same dynamic as high school, it is just a different social setting. When you're in over your head, you're in. It doesn't matter if it's Danny the track star or Meg Ryan, if the swingers around you come from a higher vine you feel uncomfortable. The trick is to realize everyone spent as much time in front of the mirror as you did worrying about their zits or bad hair, so calm down, look at them like you know their secret. The sooner you can learn this the better.

Smile: All day or night long, wherever there is discomfort people will be tense and expecting tension in return. The best way to change this sticky chemistry is to give someone the opposite reaction than they expect, and they'll usually expect a frown. I'm not saying be Tara Lipinsky or some beauty pageant winner, but if you do make icy eye contact break it with a silly, self-effacing grin, not a condescending ear to ear fake. Showing the teeth is the easiest way to relay the love. Put it out there and see what happens.

Common Ground: If you are stuck alone with someone or stuck in line for the bathroom imagine you know the person already and tell them how much it sucks to wait in line for the bathroom, tell them about the girl you saw passed out on the front lawn and how you hope she gets home OK. It's really easy to strike up a conversation, I do it all the time, sometimes by total accident. There are times when I can't keep my mouth shut and I tell some lady on the plane how much I love her baby. Soon enough I am offering to baby-sit . . . One lady in Malibu even accepted! She never called me but she had the cutest baby. Finding common things between people is never impossible. We all came from somewhere and we're all in need of compliments or catharsis. Practice at the grocery store. If you can get the mean old man in line to open up about his daughter-in-law the dental assistant then chances are you can diffuse some party discomfort by making friends with perfect strangers.

Divide and Conquer: Take the last step, apply to twenty or thirty people there without repeating compliments or anecdotes, and you will have a hearty send-off when you leave. It only takes two good conversations to pass a lot of time at parties, so root around for some common interests and chances are you'll get something better than an ugly black hickey out of the evening, you'll share some time with a like-minded individual and forge a bond. Get out the guitar and play "Kumbaya"! I love this part!

Learn to Let Go: This one is so hard, especially when you feel too out of place and the other person knows it. You need to let go of a conversation when you can sense the other person doesn't want to be there. Unless you have something hysterically funny, so funny they'll need to be committed from the Scooby-Doo laughter, then drop the chitchat. When you feel you're sucking the very life force from a body then for God's sake *let it go!!!* One of the biggest party faux pas is holding someone hostage in a conversation they don't want to be a part of. If you do this they'll tell their friends you are a dork and a party bloodsucker and they'll all pin you down in the alley and beat you with licorice. What would you rather have, some humility and the ability to move on or licorice-blackened clothes and a tarnished reputation? You decide. I've had the vines . . . it's not good. I cornered Garth Brooks once. He's my favorite, he and Madonna. I cornered Madonna once too. They were both nice, although I've never been to Madonna's house and spent the night like I deserve to. Neither of them beat me with treats in a parking lot. Big stars don't do that.

If Worse Comes to Worst: Don't sweat it, 😊 but don't get drunk and make out with an ex-Marine either. I think that's what a lot of kittens do at parties, they get uncomfortable, they get drunk, and then some sailor convinces them to lift their skirt up and a puppy comes out nine months later. Is that any way to enjoy a party? What about good conversation, genuine laughter, and a moment shared between some insecure party-goers?

Next time you go to a party, whether it's your first time or the best time so far try having a little different attitude. It's not going to kill you to be uncomfortable for a few minutes. It takes a little bit to warm up to any gathering. It's like wearing sunscreen your first few days in Hawaii. If you don't take time to blend and acclimate you'll get burned. Go slow, go easy, be yourself, and remember, it's your party!

ThE Neck

There once was a girl, as these fables often start out, who had pert ankles, slender tendons, a pampered pooper, and a kind, turtle-like smile. Her only flaw, if these things can be termed "flaws," was an unusually thick, meaty neck. I've often wondered whether the meat was gristle or muscle, but this story was told to me by someone who knew her well, the same someone whose sister's boss had his kidneys removed in a hotel room in Las Vegas and whose friend's mother had glitter on her nether regions and showed it off with oblivious zest to the gynecologist, and apparently this detail was irrelevant or too foggy to recall off the bat. We'll call her The Neck.

The Neck was an intellectual, an athlete, and a socialite who had reason, or so one would think, to love a lot of aspects of her life and herself. Have you ever seen a turtle smile? It's glorious! Instead she would pace around nervously between javelin throws, Longfellow readings, and cotillions. She would stammer and complain endlessly about how loathsome her fat neck was (fat? she could have been an exaggerator) and how difficult it was to live a life among the perfect with a chubby, wrinkly neck. Those are not my words, apparently they came directly from her mouth. She was a fantastic cook, a world-class markswoman, a mathlete . . . do you think these had any bearing on how she saw herself? She was, when she wasn't droning on and on about her turkey fat, a delightful conversationalist, a decorated humanitarian, and a keen chess player. If I had *one* of these brilliant qualities there is no way on God's green fairway I would do anything but pat myself on the back. Markswoman? What teenage princess knows how to shoot a rifle or semiautomatic weapon? Her genius is unparalleled. Whatever.

The Neck came from a good home. Her father was a pharmaceutical representative who traveled infrequently enough that he was a known presence in their house, and he had hands that would make Paul Bunyan blush with inadequacy. Huge. *Huge!* He could cup Dolly Parton's bosom until it disappeared (and rumor has it he tried it once as a youth in Nashville). Her mother was an activist for the Birds of Pray foundation, a group of secularists who wanted children to pray in school to no one in particular. Other than weekly meetings and an occasional lecture at community colleges and technical schools, The Neck's mom was a proud and nurturing homemaker, maybe a little off base, but still a force of compassion in a world without maternal beacons. Her mom was shapely and tall, definitely gave her good ankles to The Neck, but she had a very long set of legs. Some say she had an eighth of a midsection, practically all gams, but she looked swingin' in a dress so no one complained. The Neck noticed her mother's slender, ostrich-like neck, yummy in its delicacy and form, taut and fancy. It made her cry in the shower. She'd lift the folds on her own neck and sob. The Neck could be a bit dramatic when she wanted to be.

Between training for the marathon and a night of brawling and boozing with the chess club (The Neck *always* drank seltzer and cranberry juice), The Neck found herself cavorting with a few of her classmates in the mall, trying on shoes at Penney's and eating Shamrock Shakes, when the conversation grew quiet. As obsessives often do when the attention isn't on them for two seconds, The Neck looked at her friends The Cheerleader and The Sperm Bank and said, "You guys, do you think I have a fat neck?" The Sperm Bank choked on her sputum, the only fluid in her mouth at the time, and The Cheerleader said enthusiastically, "Ohmygod . . . noooooo! You are so cute and smart! It's not small like mine, but you are still sooooooo cute!" Comforting words they were not. The Neck saved the moment. "Yeah, forget about it. Let's just move on." "Exactly," said The Sperm Bank, dead set on the next destination. "Let's just find some cute guys and make out with them in the arcade." And so they were off, short skirts a-swingin', songs a singin', three ladies in a mall, two of them intellectually inferior to The Neck, happy as a pack of cigarettes in a gangster's jacket.

They saw these three hot guys standing by Orange Julius, all varsity and stylish with cool oozing out of their loafers. The Sperm Bank, dying to live up to her name and reputation, strutted right over to them and said, "Hey." They said, "Hey. Wanna party?" And so they all walked around the mall together, six teenagers in heaven, thinking naughty thoughts, obeying all the rules of cool. Slick. And so they sat eye to eye on a picnic-style table, The Neck across from The Homicidal Maniac, The Sperm Bank across from The Open Sore, and The Cheerleader face-to-face with The Interior Designer, chatting themselves into lust or boredom, when all of a sudden the pressure of being the best at everything from orthodonture to athletics snapped The

Neck like a dried-out reed in the hands of a sailor. If you were listening to her vibe you would have heard the *crack!* from miles away. Simultaneously her father slammed his fist down on a counter in an office building where they buy pharmaceuticals, her mother ran out of the house and just kept on running, praying out loud to no one in particular, and The Neck started in on herself. "My neck is so big. Do you know what it's like to have a neck this big? Starving children in Africa would rather starve, I'm sure, than have to deal with such an impediment their whole lives. I have to wear turtlenecks in August, I will never fit into one of those fashionable chokers, and people always look at me like I'm a circus freak. I hate my neck! It sucks so bad! I hope I work with the blind someday, yeah, blind people who can't see my fat, freaky neck!!!" The Homicidal Maniac, who was a bit odd, really, heard nothing but the sound of gerbils skittering around in his head like shifty rodents. The noise. Mama. He had to kill the gerbils. He had to kill The Neck. "Wanna take a walk?" he managed between silent screams and the taste of sewer. "Sure, why not!" So they strolled, leaving behind their friends' conversation about jute rugs and monkey sex. Apparently The Neck's diatribe had fallen on deaf, lustful ears.

And away they walked, past Cinnabon, through the parking lot, into a field. Normally The Neck wasn't so suggestible, but after her mondo breakdown she felt she could use some fresh air and a sympathetic shoulder to whimper on. She felt cold. Her good instincts, the ones that told her not to buy the turquoise lamé wallpaper for her bedroom, had somehow failed her. The Homicidal Maniac began walking toward her, his lifeless hazel eyes not quite as fetching under the fading sun. He staggered and winced. Was he crying? No! He was sweating so bad it was making his Salon Selectives gel drip into his eyes. He raised his leathery hand and slapped The Neck. "Why?" she cried like Reese Witherspoon would in that movie with Marky Mark. "Because you talk too much, and the gerbils." He raised both hands, she cowered, he saw the glistening porky flesh, ripe for a hearty wrenching. It danced before him, that neck, like a toddler listening to the Spice Girls, young and unashamed. Boldly he tried to grasp that horrible, fat neck, only to be met by an awkward slipping sensation. She too was sweating and her neck was *huge!!!!* He tried again to take her down; this tree would succumb because he was The Lumberjack. The resistance was uncanny. The Neck could feel he was *trying* to choke her, but somehow the object of her hatred, her unwanted candidate for liposuction, was saving her life. The terrier in her jolted away from him, the mere surprise of it threw him back. He lunged again but her dogs were barking all the way up the hillside. She ran far, far from The Homicidal Maniac, through the parking lot, into the mall, and to the nearest pay phone to call the Proper Authorities. The Homicidal Maniac laboriously stumbled back into the mall, not really thinking too clearly. He could focus only on neck, The Neck. He wanted to choke the life from her, but that was impossible because her neck was *gigantic!!!!* By the time he found her again she was shrieking with joy at surviving the jaws of death, and as ladies are want to do she compared his hands with her father's and laughed aloud at their puny size. Wimp, wuss, midget hands. The Law Enforcement Officer took The Neck's testimony, The Paper took her picture, and The Homicidal Maniac was finally brought to justice. A serial killer on the lam who met his match in the mall. A lady with excellent cardiovascular capabilities, a terrific knack for conversation, and one hell of a neck. The Neck.

The moral of this tale is this—next time you find yourself complaining about saddlebags, sparse eyelashes, unsightly back hair, or thick feet, just remember that may be the attribute that saves your life in the mall. Remember The Neck.

Kennedy

tHE Eyes HAvE it

I love people-watching. If someone put a lifestyle questionnaire in front of me right this minute I would probably list people-watching as one of my top five activities. I can get lost in fantasizing about people's lives, why that guy is wearing a blue short-sleeve shirt, why he cut his sideburns all the way off, why he put on a pair of old Hush Puppies. I wonder how much thought they put into their appearance and how self-conscious they are, if they're from Florida, and if they know I'm looking at them. I live for mumblers and gigglers, peculiar old men, washed-up divas. I must say the best place in the continental U.S. for people-watching has to be New York City. I could spend hours on the subway chatting with businesswomen about Martha Stewart and the monopoly she has on domestic uselessness, laughing with an obese immigrant about the joy of good lasagne. The subway is heaven. I could ride it all day long waiting for my wings. The best thing to do with a New Yorker is to get into a full-fledged afternoon staring match. I think they invented it. In the Big Apple staring is not a way to make

71

simple eye contact, it is a means of communication to protect your mojo and let someone know you are either a) too tough to mess with, b) completely indifferent and are looking right through them, or c) sexually attracted to them in a very dirty way and plan on following them all the way to Seventy-third Street. If someone gives you c) you immediately must counterattack with a). The point of a subway stare-off is to convey everything with one hearty, piercing stare. If you keep looking at the poindexter nervously as if you are checking in on a sleeping baby then you have lost the game. It's that simple. I like to play with five or six people on one train and see if I can be the one to look away last. This can be tough. I've held a good optometric grip for up to five minutes and it hurts. If your eyes water from keeping them open too long and tears fall out you're as good as dead. Crying like a sissy is like waving the surrender flag. A no-no in NYC.

     Maybe that's why I liked living in New York right off the bat. It was a visual challenge, a chance to be an ambassador and a tyrant all at the same time . . . in complete silence! Eyes are such useful devices and when we realize their power we can capture a situation or a man with a lingering look and destroy him when we glance away, as if to say, "Sorry, you had your chance to flirt and you blew it." Men are so vulnerable to a good stare—it's just too honest for them. It's also the best way to see what's going on. A stare can be a **standoff,** a way of establishing momentary superi-

Caught in a staring contest standoff. (Greg DeBoer)

ority without having to embarrass yourself by saying something stupid. This is usually done in a dead-ahead stare with face muscles relaxed and both eyes three quarters of the way open looking directly into either one eye or right between the two. If you have your eyes open too wide or if you let them wander then you look too intense and psychotic. You can be relaxed and focused all at the same time and it creates a wall. Don't bother with the standoff if you have pinkeye, allergies, or sunglasses on. It blows the

Here, I'm withering some snotty salesperson with the sizeup stare. (Greg DeBoer)

effect. You can give someone the **sizeup,** which is useful against exgirlfriends, snotty retail salespeople, and anyone who deserves a going-over. With this you pull the head farther back from the body, hands on hips, and take the creature in with your gaze, going from head to toe, down and up and down again with a bit of a smirk. It's a snotty move but establishes snobby superiority when necessary. If it's your boyfriend's overly flirtatious ex use the same technique with tons of ice. Brrrr . . . I think I need a sweater. If you've gone too far and need to apologize to your boyfriend just give him **the coquettish puppy.** This is with the chin tilted downward, mouth corners pushed back slightly, and sorry eyes wide

I can be a coquette, too. It's all in the eyes. (Greg DeBoer)

73

This is the glare.
(Greg DeBoer)

open. **The dart** is a short piercer that catches people so off guard they're likely to fall right over if they've skipped a meal. This is intense eyes, a furrowed brow, and a quick, piercing *snap!* It's sort of the exclamation look, great for someone who's just blown a secret. You have to know someone really well in order for this to work, they have to know you mean business. There's the dart's slightly longer counterpart, **the glare,** which instantly conveys disdain and should be executed with eyes squeezed contemptuously to half mast as if to force evil thoughts from your head and get a clear picture of whomever you despise all at once. If you hold this one too long you look like you're straining to read, not mulling over nasty thoughts. Your eyes can be used as a **sexual showdown.** This one is similar to a standoff, only with a cocked eyebrow and a more welcoming expression, as you are thinking naughty thoughts and unashamedly letting Mr. Resistor know you are debating sucking his tongue into the back of your throat. This is a tremendous tactic that allows him to sniff the fumes of your desire without choking on the obviousness of tacky come-on lines, short skirts, or dangerous promises. If you are using the showdown he needs to feel

And finally, my version of the showdown. (Greg DeBoer)

74

your irises meet, there has to be a spark between you that goes right into your heart and belly. Again, boys love the feeling but they aren't sure what to do about it because it's too subtle to act on immediately and too easy to deny if his bragging gets out of line. Eyes are sexy and need to be stimulated. You've heard all the mumbo jumbo about men needing strippers and porn because their visual nature requires frequent and consistent stimulation. Think how powerful it is for an eye to be stimulated by another eye: The very thing that's seeing someone is turned on by what's looking at them. Ooooooh, shivers just thinking about it.

I think I used to abuse the stimulus by penetrating men in inappropriate situations. For example, when a teacher was trying to scold me for writing an overly sexual report on testicular cancer I was giving him a faux innocent Lolita showdown, a melter and scorcher with aloof and girlish overtones. If you use this one in the wrong place it can be mean, mean, mean. Men respond too quickly to a teenage ingenue. I loved staring at guys when I was younger. I guess the word *staring* implies blank discomfort and wallflower confidence, but I loved looking at boys who interested me in a way that was a little too intense. Instead of riding the subway I was riding the man train, the naked dirty man train that was all in my head. Stare for sport, it's fun! Guys do it all the time in a more overt fashion, unable to hide their lust. Why can't we do it to open them up and reveal just a peep of ourselves? If nothing else you'll be able to tell whether his eyes are really hazel or you just imagined them that way.

These times of ours are very awkward. It's hard for ladies to get a word in edge-wise. Ladies are much better listeners, so why not use that innate observation to stare and communicate in a different way? You want to flirt with a boy? Keep your skirt on and reach into his eyes instead of his pants. No one ever got pregnant from holding a look too long. Today it pays to be creative and it feels better to stare into the future rather than get railroaded in your sleep. Just don't blink—you might miss the moment.

ThE *Hour* oF *Power*

How do you keep the moments from drifting away without any meaning or acknowledgment? How do you capture your youth so that it will never leave you? How do you take advantage of precious energy and priceless years? This world gets so complicated with its technological obsession and its uninspirational soul-stealing and greed. There is, however, an answer to the thorny bitterness that can get the best of us down. There is a big guy who cares. He is willing to give us his undivided attention, his caring thoughts, and a crisp one-hundred-dollar bill if we're lucky. I know this man as well as my own father, but I've never met him. I have heard tales of his grace and compassion from people who have briefly entered his realm only to return richer and to share their own inspirational tales of salvation. That man is Bob Barker and his show is the most consistent and thoughtful program on television. It's . . . *The Price Is Right!!!!!*

I'll never forget the first time I was touched by his wisdom. My grandmother had paid us a visit from Brownstown, Indiana. We were passing time one morning in May when her gentle hand fiddled with

the remote until the screen glowed perfectly. A man with black, impervious hair appeared in a crisp suit holding a long, narrow microphone, a sort of magic wand. I watched as the show unfolded, delighted to be a part of the money exchanges and the constant tension. It was all so simple . . . so . . . so . . . *alive!* I was hooked.

The game starts like this. An announcer (the current man is Rod Roddy, although there have been a few others) belts out his boundless joy as he tells us the name of the show. The camera teases us as it pans the audience back and forth, up and down, revealing the bright colors of the studio and the eager faces  in the crowd. Rod plucks out four lucky soldiers chosen to do battle for the great General Barker, the host of our show, the savior of our day. Bob sharpens the contestants, forces them to think, and if he really likes them he makes some disparaging comment about their last name or home town. He stopped making racial slurs a long time ago. The four people with their price tags/name tags all run up to a panel four across and are given an item to bid on, such as a lamp or a set of porcelain Dalmatians from Mexico, and whoever bids closest without going over gets to go up onstage with Bob and play their own game. The show is a playground for everyman, the members of society who fight so hard for each dollar they earn. It's their chance to win riches just by knowing what it takes to make a purchase in today's tough economy.

Now, the point of being in contestants' row is to bid as close to the item as possible without going over. Once in a while a wily contestant gets through the ranks and throws a curveball for everyone. He may think the other three contestants have overbid, in which case he will bid only *one dollar*. I love this part! I usually stand up and pump my fists in a show of solidarity for the brave juggernaut who just put his whole life on the line. One time I had so much adrenaline going I chewed a rut into my hand the size of a xylophone baton. It didn't get infected, but it was a really great story. Whatever the person bid is immediately put onto a screen in front of them so we at home don't have to write everything down. So here you have three yahoos who have just bid $16,000 on a Pez dispenser that looks like David Hasselhof and the charming smirker who maybe hates *Baywatch* or is bitter they took *Knight Rider* off the air just thumbed his nose at America and the entire free world by bidding only one dollar. *One friggin' dollar!* Another contestants' row fast one is to bid a dollar higher than the person next to you if you think their bid is close but maybe a little too low. This is also risky, but when the person gets it right the place goes wild. I heard a lady had a heart attack from such an incident and was resuscitated by the Big Man himself, Bob Barker, lover of animal sterilization and knower of CPR. These are the positives, the sweet nothings that can turn a usually ho-hum part of the show into game seven of the World Series.

There are some shenanigans I *will not* put up with on contestants' row, particularly when people get up to bid and they turn around to get advice from their kin and fellow seamen. Hey! People! This is a show for the strong and independent, it is a perfect example of manifest destiny, a daily illustration of the American dream, not some communal showboating. This kind of crap holds up the entire show and makes Bob feel rushed and irritable. I suggest if you are ever fortunate enough to make a trip to Television City, California, you don't waste Mr. Barker's time by turning around like a weak baby mouse searching for your mother's teat in need of a suckle, it's not good for America.

Anyway, whoever gets picked plays a game and whether they win or lose the cash in Plinko or the Daihatsu in the supermarket game they *all* get a chance to participate in the Showcase Showdown because Bob is *fair*. He wouldn't invite you into his home just to humiliate you even if you embarrass yourself by adding an extra thousand dollars onto the price of the his and her ATV's. The point of the Showcase Showdown is to pick two very fortunate people who will get their every wish granted by having the world's finest treasures and trips paraded before them by Barker's Beauties. The Beauties are a sight . . . a collection of models and pageant winners who silently show off all the goods whenever goods are to be shown off during initial bidding, the games, and the show's most glorious moments . . . the unveiling of the showcases. If you are setting your sights on becoming one of Barker's Beauties you'd better rethink your career choices. It's easier getting a Supreme Court appointment. In fact, Sandra Day O'Connor had a shot at it but blew her audition so badly she went back to law school. Rumor has it she's still licking her wounds and refuses to watch the show. Anyway, the Showcase Showdown gives all the winners from contestants' row a chance to spin a big sparkly wheel that has numbers on it from $.05 to $1.00. The point is in two spins to get as close to a dollar as possible without going over. You want to reach up and pull down in an even, sweeping motion so the wheel has a chance to go around at least once, *one full time,* or Bob gets *pissed*. One time I was

80

sure he was going to head-butt this woman from Kansas so hard she would have to have her jaw rewired, all because she wouldn't spin the wheel hard enough. Now don't make him mad. For crying out loud, this man has been at it for a long time and he doesn't need weaklings ruining his mood so early in the day. OK?! Jesus. If you get the one dollar in one try you get to spin for five or ten thousand dollars and immediately win a spot in the showcase, boom, no questions asked, thank you, governor. It's like a metaphor for our fine country, a little bit of skill and a whole lotta luck combined with second chances give you ample opportunity to win some crap and look like an ass doing it. And they said patriotism was dead.

By the time the show gets to the displaying of the showcases I am usually in a sugar coma or have taken another run at sleep, and unless someone wins both showcases (an *extremely* rare occurrence), I don't really watch the end of *TPIR*. Like I once heard in an Aerosmith song, "life's a journey, not a destination." Translation: Bob's musings are not a means to an end, rather a prism by whose light we can all measure ourselves, and along the way, as we catch a glimpse, we can become changed and ultimately better. At :59 minutes when the Good Man goes on his liberal diatribe about having your pets spayed and neutered I have been long bathing in the foreplay of orgasmic contestants' joy, I've basked in the bright light of the United States' longest-running game show, I have choked on the nectar of liberty, I have idealized the portrait of masculinity Mr. Barker has set and demanded that the men in my life live up to those standards, and I love me a little more. Some folks say we Barker Thumpers are a tad obsessive. I say, "Why fight it?" And then I sleep a glorious slumber, preach the good word, wake up, and do it again for the General. Amen.

Turkey Breast

What the hell are you gonna do, have plastic surgery? Put a couple of plastic saline packets in your chest so some lobotomized boy toy can get off on your fun bags? Please! Every breast size has its advantages, so don't be bummed out if you are not Pamela Anderson by the time you are fourteen. As I've said before, the really, really cute girls in junior high (remember The Chicken Theory) always turn out either fat or strippers, so be thankful you are among the underdeveloped. Talk to any chesty girl you know and chances are they will confess their envy at your lack of endowments. I think most plastic surgery for fake boobs is pretentious and sad, and I wish all girls who felt they weren't dealt an ample enough hand would take up running or something, or just watch chesty Betsy try and play softball with a triple D cup. It's not easy.

I was the prime minister and queen of the underdeveloped nations in junior high and high school, but somehow after years of feeling sorry for myself I have realized that my situation isn't that bad. When you are flat-chested you always look a little bit skinnier because your clothes don't puff out with too much mammarial padding. When you get pregnant you can stay upright, unlike girls with too much weight upstairs, who tend to tip over like a sleeping cow after a truck-load of farm boys have had their way with her. Large-breasted women tend to have a little more difficult time once they get pregnant because

their breasts ache and swell and generally are a lot less comfortable. See? Even though your calf-birthing years are far, far ahead of you (I hope) you now have something to look forward to once you're ready to rear a few chilluns.

Can you tell I don't stuff my bra?

As for now, you probably want to fit in that prom dress or clingy sweater or bikini top and want some milk sacks to get the boys ex-cited. You should instead think about accen-tuating your accentuatable parts. You may not have the Grand Tetons (that is a moun-tain range in Wyoming, not the name of an adult film), but who is to say your abs can't be the kind to make Janet Jackson feel meager? Stay in shape because it makes you feel a little bit better. I've always had cart-pulling, eastern European legs. The kind of legs my Romanian an-cestors had so they could still plow the fields when the ox died. They were good for waterskiing and biking, and a few jock boys coveted my quads and told me I would be a good running back if I had any speed. I tried to stay in shape and do my best with what I had control over, everything from my biceps to my posture to flossing at night, because you just don't have any control over the radio knobs God gives you.

As far as stuffing goes, I am for it as long as it prevents you from going the surgical route. Stuffing is now an accepted part of the major beauty pageants (not that *they* are role models for a well-adjusted self image). Fake boobies serve no purpose other than masturbatory material for secretly misogynistic vampires who ultimately want you tied up and subservient or pregnant with their seed. Do I sound bitter? It's only because in seventh grade this kid Cole shouted from across the room, "Why don't you come over here. My desk is getting a little bumpy and I could use your chest to write on." True story. Ouch. That is why I say if all rational options have been exhausted, then stuff it like a turkey, ladies! Do it instead of surgery and because it gives your body a little better proportion, not so Bobby Bra Watcher has something to spank it to . . . that is not what you're for. Force him to like you for all of your magical assets, whether they be physical or intellectual.

My suggestion is to get a few nicely (not over the top) padded bras so your bustline remains pretty consistent and not noticeably changed. Toilet paper and socks get so lumpy (remember *Are You There, God, It's Me, Margaret?*). That way you will have a little ego padding to set your mind at ease and you can get on to bigger and better things like how to get the principal fired. Next time you feel envy creeping up in your stomach because Julie Juggs is having all the fun, just picture her in five years drowning in gallons of tears and a boyfriend in prison. Believe you me, you are one of the lucky ones who got a late and better start.

Turkey Breast

hOW <u>Not</u> tO gEt
a Man

Oh God! On this I could write a whole book. This is a topic I know about and this is the kind of advice I am overqualified to give. If I had an M&M for all the needless heartache and worthless desperation I went through before I found my prince I would have enough to fill a wheelbarrow and I could wash them down with a bushel of tears. Speaking of M&M's, in a time of hormonal need my heartstrings played for a redheaded jock named Wade. Wade was phenomenal, average build, medium height, limited vocabulary . . . I was breathless. I would try and steal a word with Wade every chance I got, passing him in the hallway, skipping fifth period because I knew he had independent study in the library, driving past football practice. Oh yes!—I was subtle. Finally I devised a plan, a silly, thoughtless, painfully obvious plan with holes as big as the end of a Tampax Super Plus applicator. I knew Wade (doesn't the name alone remind you of walking through a cesspool?) had a foreign language fourth period because I passed him every day coming out of my French class third period. I lugged about

87

six quarts of peanut M&M's around in a goofy collegiate drinking mug thinking, "Oh, I know! Wade will stop me and want to eat my M&M's, at which point he'll notice my painted mouth and make out with me in the hall before his German class." Well, that didn't happen. Instead I got a bunch of dirty looks from some older girls and a reputation as a diabetic. Wade never acknowledged me, not that day, not that school year, not even after we graduated from high school and I worked on TV.

There was another sad time when I had fallen for an Adonis . . . he was the state's very finest javelin thrower. His name was Bart. I happened upon Bart at a huge statewide outing where kids from different high schools participated in mock-legislature, passing bills, debating issues. Either Bart was there lobbying to allow monosyllabic athletes equal rights, or he was one of those guys who wanted to seem "well rounded" to the prospective colleges and universities he was planning on gracing. I got ahold of his phone number in the directory handed out at the end of the "session" so all the little future lawmakers could keep in touch with one another. Yeah, I called him . . . *about five hundred times!!!!* And that went over well. It's as if he was playing his part perfectly in the script of my life where I faced constant rejection from the sportos of the world. Bart pretended not to remember me when I called; what a fitting name for that young man. After the five hundred and first time either the steroids were kicking in or my plan of self-humiliation was working, because he pretended not to have gone to the fake congress thing at all. For most that would be a hint, that would be the clue that *maybe* it was time to move on to another stick-throwing freak, but no. I had to keep going. A few days later my brother Brian came out of his convulsive laughter long enough to tell me that one of Bart's javelin buddies from my high school got wind of my mild flirtation with stalking and told his mother, who called my mother to request that I stop calling Bart immediately—it was upsetting the community. There was only one thing left to do . . . for $7.95 I bought a used wedding dress at a thrift store, bought a six-pack of Robitussin, took the bus to Bart's house, and sat in the rain crying for seven hours. OK, that's not true, the wedding dress was borrowed and I was only there for about seventeen to eighteen minutes. The moral of the story is if you want to be like me and spend as little time as possible with a boy who is interested in you, then follow these quick and painful steps:

As soon as eye contact is established with a boy you like immediately **begin talking incessantly** about things that are of little or no interest to him. Possible subjects: your period, past failed relationships, bodily fluids. **Find out his phone number and call.** *A lot.* If a woman (i.e. his mother, sister, girlfriend) answers either giggle and hang up *or* be extra pushy and demanding and leave your phone number each time. If he answers strike up a conversation and don't let it end, even if it means a two-hour Friday night filibuster. **Find out where he lives and drive by** five or six times within any given hour. Leave cute notes on his car. If one of his *women* spots you glare at them and peel out. If he sees you stall your car by popping the clutch out too soon. **Let all his friends know** how you feel about him. Don't be afraid to embellish a little and say you guys got engaged over the weekend. I did this to a guy a couple of years ago. No wonder his sister bitch-slapped me at that Hanson concert! **Walk past him and talk about him really loud** with your friends. Make up things about how he tried to kiss you when you walked by with M&M's and how he said you were his *special* little muffin maker.

If these don't work well enough I'm sure you can think up your own. Oh, and remember, it helps if you fall for the wrong man. Try someone who is either way too old for you or a guy in a band with a drug habit who just got out of jail. Who doesn't love a good challenge?

Hormone Rush

Do you hear the rhythmic beats of jungle music coming from your belly? Does the rat-tat-tat of a snare drum drift up from somewhere inside your skirt? Do you want to French-kiss the dangerous-looking thug in home economics and dry-hump your geometry teacher? Behold the bug, you've been taken hostage by your hormones. When I was fifteen I was a walking hormone, obsessed with males, kissing, sex, dirty words, innuendo, saying the word "boner," talking about tampons. It was a bit nerve-racking. Tempting as it was to act on all these primal instincts, I think I was somehow too obnoxious for the freshman and sophomore guys. They were steeping their teabags in the bath of testosterone, and I was set afire with my own self-expression, a little too "keyed up" for the athletic supporter crowd, but man was I rarin' to go. It is so cruel to have your ovaries fired up like a pimped-out 74 Mustang with dual exhaust and have the same chemicals that make lovin' fun also make you break out in a less than appetizing display of irrational comments and acne. What is the human body designed for? Torture?

I'm sure in the olden days when maidens were dragged by their hair into caverns it was pretty convenient to menstruate at twelve or thirteen—people were only living into their mid-forties. Even after the time of King Tut when the wagons were pulling into the new frontier it was nice to have an able-bodied young woman with broad hips and sturdy legs ready to give birth seventeen or eighteen times. You had to get going by fourteen or fifteen so the old man had a receptacle for his tadpoles and enough offspring to help on the farm. But now? When women are not around just to squirt out another junior because a farmhand died and another body was needed for Amish League softball, why are our bodies still starting out so soon and crapping out so fast? Is evolution ever going to catch up to the climate of the late twentieth century? Probably not, but it certainly is nice to have the energy

to daydream about sex when you're young. Life is cruel . . . you can be so homely and underdeveloped at one age and so desperately in need of a good smooching, and the next minute you're thirty-five with three kids, less libido, and no time to act on it when you are in the mood. So just start having sex now while you have the energy and opportunity, while you really, really want it! No, just kidding. There are ways to accept your hormone level while allowing your integrity and better judgment to prevail. Without that judgment high school would be a big swingers' club and people would be walking around completely naked in the halls playing grab ass and feed the kitty in between classes. I'm sure some of those liberal private schools do that, those hooligans.

At seventeen KiKi and I were the only remaining virgins in our class. In her case it was in part due to her religious upbringing, which taught that having sex was just wrong and against God's will. I chose to remain intercourse-free because it didn't seem prudent to go around risking pregnancy at sixteen or seventeen when you could have just as much fun doing other things (you know, like knitting or volunteering at animal shelters). It seemed a lot more fun not to have sex than to have to worry about getting a sitter or running out of food stamps to buy diapers nine months later. Boys love to tease you when you won't have sex. *Do you know what you're missing?* Yes, diseases and children. *How can you not have sex?* Easy, I don't put other people's penises in my missy. *Sex feels so good!* Yeah, so does my self-respect three days later when you don't call. Boys will do a lot of dumb things, like *say* they had sex with you just for giggles and to impress their friends. Boys will say anything. I dated a fat-faced rich boy once who drove an outdated BMW and smelled like fresh cat pooh. He took me to a really stupid concert and I pretended it was the best night of my life. He slow-danced with me and I kissed his neck. It tasted like scallions. We went back to his house where he bored me with tales of his housekeeper being on vacation and nearly put me to sleep with his family photo album. When the uneventful kiss came around and we rolled around on the floor for a while all I could think about was calling KiKi and telling her about my dismal night. He took me home, heartily impressed with his boring car (show me a man with a Chrysler and I'll show him affection) and lame, rehashed stories, and finally dropped me off. The obligatory kiss goodnight, the "Oh yeah, boring guy, it was swell," and I was off to bed, trying to rid my senses of cats and onions. That punk never called me again but he was kind enough to go back to his high school and tell anyone who would listen how easy I was and how we had sex all night. Oooooh, yuck! He was the poster boy for why I saved myself. The story ends well. The Chicken Theory works for both genders. Mr. Dry Hump BMW went on to become unpopular, bloated, and unemployed. My hormones certainly got the better of me that night, but I didn't shed any clothes or give up the hey-nanny-nanny. So thankful, so thankful.

I get really bummed out when I hear supposedly all-knowing adults proclaiming the golden rules and keys to life. *You shouldn't have sex because it is wrong, children!* No, you should respect yourself and make decisions based on how you see yourself and how you want others to see you. I personally had a hard time giving my virginity away so young because a) the baby and disease thing and b) sex to me is ultimately an expression of great love, and although I had bouts with serious judgment-bending lust I had never had a true *love* when I was a teenage party princess. I was too busy fantasizing about my science teacher and flirting in the hallways. The idea that sex was a gift you were given and can never take back really struck me, because I'm a Virgo and I hoard things by nature. I have boxes of shoes and nice stationery that are still waiting for the perfect occasion before they'll get used. You think I gave up my virginity because a guy had nice eyes and he told me he was only going to put it in for a second? Please . . . I'd rather be ridiculed by the heat-seeking missile boys looking for a silo.

Next time your hormones act up on you just remember it is a

chemical reaction in your body set up to tell cave girls it was time to mate because fourteen used to be midlife. Procreate in good time, find a nice career path, and set yourself up before you get married. Children are the most beautiful gift on the planet, but don't become a baby with a baby. You'll end up destroying your self-esteem and resenting your child. Take your time experiencing everything and don't try to force your way into adulthood. It will be here soon enough and it's all one big pain in the ass anyway. Live with your parents, party down with your friends, and don't be ashamed to save yourself for later or for someone you really love. As Ian Mackaye would tell you (I think), self-control is the most punk rock thing in the world. Next time you hear the rhythmic beats of hormones pounding in your ovaries and up your prom dress do yourself a favor and go dancing instead.

Prude

Being a prude in our steamy society of *Three's Company* reruns and endless douche ads used to be a bad thing. If a lady was labeled a prude she was as good as wet toast at a bruncheon, soggy and unloved. Nowadays with the Hanta virus lurking in every salty girl's hope chest boys and men alike are searching for unspoiled beauty. They want a woman with a worldly way and an unsoiled camisole. Men need prudes.

There was a time when prudedom was a life sentence of scoffing at party invitations and killing time with needlepoint and cooking casseroles  for church functions. If a woman wasn't busying herself with talking about, alluding to, or partaking in sexual intercourse there wasn't much for her to do. If she didn't feel shoddy she wasn't having a nice time. That isn't so in today's world. The prude of the new millennium is proud to have unmussed hair, she is unashamed at her lack of knowledge about twelve-inch vibrators and whorish trinkets. She is self-satisfied in her ability to keep world affairs straight for conversation and her panty drawer potpourri fresh for no one in particular. The modern-day prude has revolutionized restraint and once again made it socially desirable. It is OK to be a prude and hold your head up on the boulevard as if to say, "We of humble prurience and unconquerable libido find empowerment in Jane Austen and Egyptian cotton. We live for us." Kind of refreshing when so many of our sisters are getting ahead by giving head.

Prude wardrobe hasn't changed much in the last few decades or so. Hats, especially straw, are acceptable and celebrated. Visors and head wraps are appropriate during outdoor activity; a woman of this glorious nature would hate to have a sunburn be mistaken for a blush. Prudes favor long dresses in solid and floral prints. There has been a bit of a ruckus among prudes between the silly Laura Ashley set and the more modern prude who prefers black, navy, or burgundy solids that convey the right message without spoiling it with block-headed femininity. Whatever the color scheme the basic principle in dresses is still in place—hide the body and the legs, nothing too form-fitting, leave something to the imagination. Prudes also like to wear eyeglasses, not so much to correct astigmatism or nearsighted-ness—prudes certainly aren't physically predisposed to ocular mal-function—but to hide the precious eyes from Casanova bandits who try to steal a woman's essence by peering too deeply into the windows. A prude can hide a lot with a good loose-fitting dress but she conveys everything with a look. Close-toed shoes are widely accepted; bare feet are as revealing as bare breasts in a lot of minds. Shielding the big toe in the summer is like wearing a bra in a wet white T-shirt; you don't play with that kind of fire. Kneesocks, low-heeled boots, and a simple handbag go nicely with a prudish demeanor. Oh, and prudes always dress for themselves. It's something else that makes them so attractive.

Confidence oozes out of a woman who loves herself for the simplicity in her style. A prude wears nice bras so she will feel good all the way down to the barest layers. She knows men fantasize about her under-things. Although she doesn't acknowledge the fantasy she still likes to feel sexual under all that gabardine, you know, just for her.

Prudes have a definite code they follow. A lot of it is tradition but it's mostly common sense, silent codes that have to be followed in order to be a really ripe and tasteful prude. Rule number one: Prudes never talk about their panties. These are women of extraordinary self-control and character. Although there is nothing more exciting than spending sixty or seventy quality minutes at Victoria's Secret buying the sweetest undergarments in heaven's realm it is against prude law to tell every Tina, Denise, and Harriet about such intimate purchases. That kind of info could burn a girl, as it appears reckless if it gets into the wrong minds. A lot of loosey-goosey girls buy thongs and nipple-less bras just so they can tell a bunch of guys about it, only to be made fun of later at the urinal. Prudes know you don't establish respect from a man by tramping around his imagination. Prudy ladies also never talk about matters of sexual desire in mixed company. That is the cornerstone of prudism; a tight lip and a stern exterior are crucial no matter how revved up her ovaries are beneath that loose-fitting gown. It may be a facade, but letting it go can rock the very foundation of a prude and may destroy all the mystery and intrigue she has worked so hard to create. The same goes for getting drunk on the first date. If you do it with one they'll all expect it and eventually someone will get into your chastity belt, blow the whistle, and turn the key. They'll know you're not the real deal, and there is nothing worse to a man than a faux prude except a buxom hooker that turns out to be a man, but that's another chapter. It's just not good manners and it brings expectations down for the rest of us, not to mention morale and the price of love.

Prudes are usually smarter than most men, otherwise the use of reverse psychology would not be so successful. Being smarter goes hand in hand with being sensitive and perceptive, and where does perception oft rear its perky head? In the kiss! Prudes, although it seemingly defies prudish nature to think of or practice such things, are fantastic kissers, 👄 excelling in pout, gumption, capability, and desirability. Any man who dares cross the line by grabbing the moon-kissed face of a prudelet will get the surprise of his life in her lip knowledge and sensual vulnerability. He will feel the song of the siren blaring in his ear as she lets her guard down for half a moment, long enough to convey her ultimate power and short enough to snap back into reality. A stolen kiss from a prude woman warrants an automatic stinging slap in the face, because . . . hey! You don't get away with kissing a prude. A prude lady will always say, "No thank you" when she turns you down, and on the rare occasion she wants it will quietly squeal, "Yes please!" Prudes are so often misread and considered boring due to their seemingly consistent nature and controlled tendencies. What drives a woman to be a prude? Why would she skip out on the fun of sharing a slice of pie? Because within every prude is a woman who knows so well . . . if she holds out long enough she'll get the whole cake. 🍰

Hey Lady!

I went to the pool the other day to feel like a fish, get some blood into my muscles, and interact with my fellow pool-goers. They're usually a pretty antisocial crowd, since there's not much to talk about: "So, you like swimming? How well does your swim cap fit? Boy, it's wet in here, huh!" I love to chat with strangers, they're really just friends I haven't made yet. On this sunny day ☼ I changed my routine a little and went for the adult/senior citizen lap swim. All the ladies were standing around with their swim cards ready to be punched, their plastic bags filled with Lycra goodies, and the best intentions for an early afternoon's exercise. They were ready to talk, I'll tell you that much right now. I was in heaven! I can tell a lot of my soon-to-be friends think my conversation weighs on the trivial side but this gray-haired set was ready to play ball! One woman told me about the cold she had all week and heaven knows I love sharing germ stories. We rattled off symptoms and agreed this spring cold has gotten everyone down. I had it myself two weeks prior so I wasn't giving her any false sympathy. I

101

saw another sweet miss all alone in the corner so I went over and asked her about what else . . . the weather! She told me it was colder than a saloon in Anchorage and she nearly froze to death pulling the Monte Carlo out of the garage this morning. She did, however, have the great fortune of knitting herself a wool sweater two or three winters ago, so she put that on, knowing wool is practically impervious to the elements. That sent us on a free-for-all discussing gabardine, acrylic, cashmere, mohair . . . it was a delight. Everyone was in, I had finally found my social circle! I'm not sure if it's the difference in age but I'm guessing if I tried to have the same discourse with my peers I would have come up against a wall of mistrust and curt answers. People think you're trying to steal something from them. Do you know how much older women know about gardening, entertaining, flirting, board games, and fabrics? We have living encyclopedias, breathing historians, treasured museums right under our noses but we choose to ignore them every day.

We know how men of that generation were—cold, drunk, power-driven—but what about the women? How is it we have chosen to simplify such an important and complex segment of our society by slapping them with the title "Grandma"? Grandmothers are a link to our history, not only of society but family history as well. Since so many women of that generation were relegated to the home they spent the majority of their lives observing and documenting the whirlwind changes that were shaping our future right before their very eyes. Oh sure, the big men got to go to quarries and offices free from domestic concern while the women were expected to sit and watch the petunias grow while the meat loaf was browning. My paternal Grandmother

Hildegarde is ninety-one years old, and in her lifetime she has seen countless wars, the invention of the airplane, television, computer, daytime talk show, celebrity defense attorney, disposable diaper, automatic transmission, microwave oven, Internet, and Carrot Top. Do you think we ask her for the one thing she is most capable of giving, a centurial synopsis and her thoughts on the coming millennium? No, we ask for her patience, silence, and some more of those woven sea foam green washcloths to clean the meat loaf remnants with. My family gets mad at me be-

My grandmother Mima.

cause I'll sit and pester Gardy about the information age and life before feminism, I'll ask her why no other game show has the broad and spectacular appeal of *The Price Is Right.* To this she throws up her hands, to the others she gives expansive and thoughtful lectures about coping with change and maintaining your heart and morals in such a big, cold, fast moving world. What were they expecting me to ask her, "Grandma, can you please pass the potato salad?" I'll leave that nonsense to my denser relatives. I wanna know when the bomb is going to drop and what system of government is going to survive the Nuclear Age. If a network of sharp and loving grandmothers were in charge I think we'd be safe; they know the key to a bright future is knowing your past.

My friend Kevin once told me to interview my grandmother and find out what it was really like a few years ago during a real war or de-

Hey Lady!

pression. My mom's mom, Mima as she is affectionately known, is the sweetest Romanian grandmother this side of the Carpathian Alps. I used to think Mima was a docile woman with nothing but joy and tulips in her heart. That was until I voted Republican for the first time. Who knew a seventy-nine-year-old had so much to say about public policy? And who was I to question a person who fled war-torn Transylvania with three children and one suitcase in 1945 in the midst of Communist Russia's seizure of her homeland? Let's just say gun control and Ronald Reagan rarely come up over dinner at Mima's. She used to tell me how much she loved me and what a sweet girl I was. Now that I've taken a keener interest in her sensibilities all of a sudden I'm important enough to hear the family gossip, stuff that is too rich to print. My Mima knows ahead of time who's pregnant, who's fat, who's getting a divorce, and who's drinking too much. She knows what to cook for people who've never been to her house. I wouldn't have that ESP if my life depended on it. The sooner people in our family write off Mima's mental faculties the sooner she'll start baking them rhubarb pies and looking at them with a blank, geriatric stare. If they're not going to give her an open ear then why should she warn them about their impending weight gain and investment losses? I got the best thing going, family gossip, washcloths, and a clearer lock on the future.

Grandmothers know how to dress, they know how to be polite when the situation calls for it, and they can act like senile fools just so they can blurt out what they really think of someone. A person thirty years younger would have a much harder time telling Aunt Blanche she has fat arms; it sounds so much *sweeter* coming from Grandma. I hope I have as much to give my granddaughters as my grandmothers have given me. Even those quiet soliloquies attributed to passing delirium hold so much more for me than regurgitated soap opera plots. It may be Grandma's gentle way of letting me know to look out below, the bomb's gonna drop any day and I don't even have the right sweater on.

Dressing

If it were only so easy as dressing a salad to ready ourselves in the morning. For years I considered slathering myself in balsamic vinegar and bleu cheese, but opaque liquids can be so unflattering and clingy. And what a stench at high noon in early June . . . p.u. Dressing is the great temptation, the desire to be perfect for the other ladies, the need to be beautiful for the boys. With the way the dumb pony boys dress do they really deserve the extra effort? The loud debate over school dress codes is very interesting. Sure, dress codes annihilate personal expression and individual fashion freedom, but can you imagine the time and heartache you'd save in the morning? I swear I stayed home on more than one occasion because of a paltry wardrobe, fearing ridicule from the other chickens in hideous acid wash and clumpy mascara. If one of my nightmares came true and I found myself having to go back to high school, I think I'd be better prepared in the clothing department. I would dress according to my own whims instead of getting caught in the accordion of other people's inhibition and insecurity.

Adolescence is the ultimate buffet, a time in your life never to be rivaled. Later on you might find the world a tighter box that demands square nails, beige suits, and a plastic smile. By the time you are confident enough to realize your fashion potential you might have some hack of a boss with baggy eyes and a sour puss demanding less color in your life and more wattage from your soul. So hurry up, start dressing like a spaz while you still can. Any fashion mistakes you make in your teen years will be lovingly recalled and even yearned for the second you sell out to your first employer with a strict dress code.

There is one fashion school that frowns upon emulation and imitation for fashion inspiration. I say that's crap! You don't know what you love until you spend a week in a certain look. When you're in your forties it's OK to dress in the same color scheme from the pages of L. L. Bean, but for now it's safe to people-watch at street fairs and browse the lady fashion mags for colors and looks that suit your fancy. So go ahead, find your fancy! It's out there somewhere. I remember my mom brought five or six magazines home from Europe when I was in high school and I drooled over the sweaters and accessories, the thigh-highs and gloves. It was nearly impossible to replicate anything off the rack from the Brass Plum at Nordstrom, but I definitely had a few blossoming ideas. I wish I had allowed myself to be even freer and riskier, although it was kind of hard with two brothers looking over my shoulder every time I went out asking, "You're wearing that?" It took some time to get over that complex. More than once I lied as I left the house. I told them I was going to costume parties (it didn't work very well past November 1).

I wish I had older sisters. I dressed like a guy the first two years of high school because I was afraid to offend anyone. I spent two good years in sweats and collegiate T-shirts 👕. The pendulum eventually swung hard in the opposite direction as I stole plenty from my mother's closet. I think that's where I developed a fetish for suits. I love me a good suit. The time I went to Paris the only French I used successfully was *"Acceptez-vous American Express?"* Talk about people-watching— a single day of ogling over the fashion sense of French women is life-changing. It is so important to find out what you like, I can't stress that enough. Everyone has some opinion and leans toward one way of dressing. It may seem impossible and costly, but you'll latch onto your true calling with a long and hard enough search. Not too many people outside the highest economic stratosphere can afford Prada and Dolce and Gabana, so it is essential to look around in vintage and thrift shops for similar retro lookalikes of whatever you are going for and dive right in. Be careful. If you find at a young age you are attracted to handbags and shoes 👞 be forewarned that these fetishes turn into expensive obsessions and leave chocolate cravings and boy craziness dwarfed in their wake.

If you get daring and expressive enough you may go through as many as fifteen looks in one school year. It will be so much fun for you to look back and reminisce about your Goth period with the black lipstick, white pancake makeup, and sullen dourness, the hippie period with the patchouli oil, naked rafting trips, and Phish CD's, the punk rock girl phase with the global squatting tour, Sick of It All full back tattoo, and septum piercing. You'll marvel at your glamour phase, giggle at your skater fetish, and happily recall each phase as a part of a

109

process that ultimately showed each bright side you possess and let you become who you are.

The truly interesting dressers are the fashion sharks , the ones who each season must create a whole new look for themselves or else die a miserable death. I was never one of these people. I get too comfortable in one pair of pants 🔼 and, in between regular washings, wear them out over the course of a few months. The sharks are fun to watch because they are so self-conscious and meticulous. The opposite are the fashion plaster casts who find one blah look early on and stick with it for fear of falling off some imaginary cliff if they stray too far. They never change it and become faceless with their predictability. I know a pretty girl from high school who refuses to bring any energy into her wardrobe because she's stuck in some ghastly late eighties time warp with the same bob, same liquid liner, same everything. She hasn't even gained weight! She never learned what she liked or what she disliked, as if any sort of flexibility in her personal style posed a huge threat.

A fashion disaster—me in eighth grade with a grown-out flattop, braces, and a really bad scarf.

I was almost irreparably wounded at an early age. When I was in second grade I decided to go out on somewhat of a limb with a demand for red satin disco pants. Oh, they were amazing, and what a complement to my roller-skating and rainbow headbands and Mork suspenders. I could have loved those pants, and, between washings, I could have lived in them. That is until mean old Malinda came over,

110

gathered a few of her fat-ass friends in a circle around me, and started to laugh. Can you believe it? They are now, I can assure you, living a boring life of khaki and brown where a beige T-shirt from the Gap is a "crazy" purchase for them. I was demoralized, my young brow furrowed into a serious knot, tears creating dark red spots on my shiny disco frocks. Mom came to the rescue, bearing cords in hand, another fashion blow to the ego of the deprived. Oh well, I'm still hoping to bounce back and develop some more style.

People's words and thoughts are always daggers, no matter how hard you try to show them your tough shell. It is impossible to tell you to ignore what *everyone* else is thinking about you so you can tear through these years with color and glory dripping from every thread. Instead try and prioritize whose opinion is most important to you and reduce the number of people you are willing to compromise for. The ultimate goal is to dress for yourself in things you find attractive so each time you leave your house your clothes reflect who you are and what you see yourself as looking best in, not some impossible getup everyone else has already worn. Don't let them dictate who you are and how you feel. Who are "they" anyway? A bunch of stylistically impaired morons and freaks who would kill for a personal sense of what really looks good. Whether you are a shark, a Goth girl, or a prim and proper Pollyanna . . . wear your own style and live in your own clothes, between washings, of course.

111

drEssING oN ThE siDe:
A Discussion with Cindy

What a whirlwind and wonderful experience I had at MTV. The best part of my job, by far, was meeting all sorts of people and being lucky enough to make awesome friends along the way. Such a miss was Cindy Paragallo, Dutch-Italian hothead and stylist to the famous and difficult. Poor Cindy had to deal with all my fetishes and clothing hang-ups. Somehow she managed to get me assembled and camera-ready every day. Whenever I looked like a spaz on the air *believe me* it was my own doing. Cindy, Jimmy, Carolle, and Lauren tried desperately to get me into suits (somewhat successfully) and flower prints (hardly ever). Here is some fashion advice from a pro who knows the best designs come from within.

What is your occupation? I am a wardrobe stylist. My job is to dress people according to their personality, according to their demographic. **How did you get your job?** I got my job because before I was a stylist, I was a designer. Then I decided that I would much rather be dressing people

113

in things. It was more creative for me to dress people than to design clothes for farty companies. **You worked for a "farty" designer?** I worked for a farty lingerie designer. And I designed robes. They were actually pretty robes. **Not to toot your own horn.** Not to toot my own horn, it was the first time the company had a robe line and they hired me because they actually wanted to have a younger image. So they got me, because I was younger. **You got that when you were twelve?** I got that when I was nineteen. **Oh, very nice! Now, how do you go about picking clothes for people?** I pick the clothes based on a couple of different things, based on personality, what they themselves like to wear, I take that into consideration. Then I base a lot of it on what I, personally, think would look good with their body because a lot of people have false images of their own bodies. They won't wear certain things, but they certainly can, they just have these false images in their heads of what they look like. My job uses a lot of psychology because you have to make people believe that they look good, you have to convince them that fears of their bodies are basically just false and in their head. You have to help them overcome them. Then I pick clothes based upon the sets and the locations that we are shooting in, trying to make sure that they work well with their environment. I pick clothes based on my demographic and what my demographic is going to understand. **So you wouldn't put someone in a plaid wool anorak for spring break in Jamaica.** No, no, I won't do that. **OK. So, you dressed me a few times at MTV. Was I easy to dress?** Well, we worked together for a lot of years. What part of our relationship are you talking about? 'Cause when we first started working together, no, you were not easy to dress. There would be hours in that wardrobe room, minutes in that wardrobe room that felt like hours. **Was I fat?** No, you were not fat at all, but you thought you were fat. You definitely

114

wouldn't wear certain things thinking you were too big to wear them when you actually looked good in them. **Is it more fun to work with people who maybe clown around a little bit with their wardrobe?** Definitely, I love when people have a sense of humor about their wardrobe or dress certain ways for certain functions just thinking that it is fun. **How do you do that? How do you bring that sense of humor out in your clothes? How do you get that confidence?** I guess that is something that is up to the individual. At certain points in their life they are not going to have the confidence to go and do that, then one day they wake up and they are like "You know what, I can have fun with it." You dress whichever way you want to dress and whichever way is going to make you feel good about yourself. **Is that the most important thing about dressing?** Yes, that is the entire thing about dressing. You have to feel good about what you are wearing and if you feel good in what you are wearing you are gonna look good, no matter what it is. You could wear a potato sack, but if you feel like you look good in it and you are comfortable in it you are going to look good in it. It is just like being comfortable in your own skin. **Do you ever want to stop people on the street and help them with their style?** Definitely. **Has that ever happened? Have you ever gone up to somebody and said, "Oh my god, that hat and those shoes! They are awful!"** No, I have never done that. I wish that I had, but no, I have never done that. **How does one go about getting their own style?** It is a process. When you can help someone see that there are different types of clothes out there and you can introduce them to different clothing companies, different designers, that helps them along the line of developing their own sense of style. A lot of people don't really pay attention to clothes all that much. **Do you have to spend a lot to look cute?** Not at all! Definitely not. You can dress yourself out of any mall store and look absolutely adorable. It is just a matter of buying yourself a $2.00 tank top and a $5.00 skirt and then putting yourself in more expensive shoes and you can make a whole entire outfit that really looks good. Then add your little finishing touches to it. Shoes are very important. **What are four things every girl needs in her wardrobe?** Every girl needs a black dress because you never know when you are going to need one of those. A good pair of jeans that fit her well, that is a necessity. A great bra. Every girl needs a bra that makes her chest look good. Your foundations are so important. If you have a good bra you can wear any top. And a really, really, really good pair of black shoes. **What is something she could do without?** Definitely she could do without white shoes. **How can you dress to look thinner?** Black, it works for me. **How can you dress to look chestier?** You need to wear a neckline that is going to emphasize your chest a little bit, so you wear a V-neck. Then you have to wear a bra that is going to push you together a little bit. **How can you keep from looking outdated?** Basically, if you don't want to look outdated you have to dress classic and kind of plain. That is a bad way of saying it, simple would be a better way. **Is it OK to wear knockoffs?** It is fine to wear knockoffs. I wear knockoffs. **What is the best advice you could give to someone struggling with their style?** If they are not comfortable and happy with their style, then they need to take a good look at their body. Figure out what shape is going to look good on them. Once they do that it is just a matter of flattering your body. If you can find a shape that really works on your body then you are going to look good. **What do you think of hats?** I think hats are cute if you have a hat head. **Do you have a hat head?** I don't. I have a pea head. All hats kind of look funny on me. **I have a malt ball head, I should wear hats.**

i'M LatE, I'm Late . . .

There were a couple of things I was pretty good at in high school and a few more at which I was a dismal failure. One of them was dating. Just as I became a little obsessed with the opposite sex I found that trying to land a date with a boy was virtually impossible. If the rare occasion did strike when a boy would ask me out I usually fumbled my way through an awkward evening that never seemed to produce a love connection. One of those nights I saddled up next to a slightly dense cowboy 🥾 and smooched him for a good hour until I had the misfortune of reaching into his jeans and finding he had latex underwear on. I think his name was Kenny. My best friend KiKi was going out with a wrestler from another high school who made these glorious promises of double dates, dual wrestling matches, and other splendid tales. I did agree to go on such a date sporting my white denim miniskirt (a trademark that summer) and big flight attendant hair. I should have taken the first flight back to a solo Friday because this guy turned out to be a simpleton, bubble-butt jock with a bad attitude and worse breath

117

(ooooh! stank mouth . . . go home, Dorothy, go home!!!). I believe the night ended with me screaming, "Well, screw you, buddy!" in my mom's driveway. I tried to block that night out, the bickering, the vanity, the soccer rocker haircut, but it did teach me a little bit about dating and what not to do. Sadly I went on to repeat the same mistakes for years, but I guess that is part of the many rest stops on the confusing road of dating. Boys can be simple, nasty, funny, quiet, nervous, impossible, narrow-minded—wait, let me stop the list before I start sounding bitter—but if you are planning on starting a relationship you have to start somewhere, and logic dictates that this may well happen on the playing field of a date. Before you go out to the ball game let me give you a heads up on what *I* have learned *not* to do on a date.

Try to Be Perfect: I call this Barbie doll syndrome. It's the hours of primping, lip gloss, and curlers that go into the preparation. What a false way to start off a great beginning! Why on earth would you knock yourself out trying to convince someone you are Miss Georgia Peach Pie, all prim and dainty with raised pinkies and a phony-baloney "Well how do you do?" when you are really brownie à la mode? Eventually these airs are impossible to keep up and the only thing you are setting yourself up for is disappointment. So Mr. Jock Society thinks he's spending four or five hours with Martha Stewart and then you go and screw it up the next date by slipping in a fart joke after dessert. This is one of those examples where I laugh now saying, "If only I could go back, wipe off that ridiculous makeup, and lose the white miniskirt." It's just so much more fun being honest. And even if you don't know yourself completely yet, go out as the side you like to be, not some impossible caricature you'll never live up to (although I still love a good smathering of lip gloss).

Bad-Mouthing: I know it's easy to find conversational "filler" in other people's flaws but it really takes away from a good time you could be having talking about better things. All this says about you is that you are either unhappy with your own life or you are so uncreative and uninspired that you are willing to drag others down, and who wants to spend time with that? Yes, it's easy to do, and it's a reliable crutch, but do yourself a favor and just voice the good stuff. I'm sure Mr. Right Now can deal without the details of your loathing.

Dominate the Conversation: Few adolescent dates did I make without bowling the other forgettable party over with my opinions on everything. I could talk and talk and talk and still have more jokes, anecdotes, and embellishments. In order to go further in any kind of relationship you need a connection, and in order to make a connection you need to share, and you can't share a thing without the other person chiming in. Without being Larry King, ask Jimmy So-and-so about himself, where did he grow up, does he have any scars, any brothers and sisters, what's his middle name, how tall is he. Make it fun, not an interrogation. Try and ask questions that don't have yes or no answers. If you can see he's not comfortable talking about himself don't keep badgering him, let him get used to you. If it helps, go to a movie early on in the night so you two get used to sitting next to each other. Plan on dinner after that so there is something to talk about for a good hour or so. I know these are terribly predictable activities, but how do you think they got so popular? Movies? Good. You don't have to talk, still together. Dinner? Great, even if it's homemade. Food, the man's heart, you know the scenario, just don't kill the scene by not letting him get a word in edgewise.

Starve: A guy will never look at a girl who is nibbling through her field greens and go "Oh, what a lovely figure! Such a dainty eater!" This one comes from my brother, who says guys *hate* when girls don't eat. You're supposed to chow in front of a guy. It lets him know you are healthy, adventurous, and unafraid of new challenges. If you eat too little it sends the message you don't think enough of yourself and you deserve to starve. Even if you're too nervous to eat a lot *never* order just a salad. He'll be more impressed if you eat pizza. You'll never get points for the rabbit food.

Laugh at Everything: I know the thinking: "Men are like dogs, insecure and in need of a good genital lick," but laughing at every story of his from how he got his penis stuck in the fire huffer to how his grandmother had a stroke at Cousin Enoch's wedding just makes you look kind of, well, kind of dumb. It makes you look shallow and indiscriminate. Jokes and stories are like fine wines, you need to pick and choose which ones you really like. If something is mildly amusing then give him a tart chuckle, if it's the funniest thing you've ever heard then let loose with a hearty guffaw, spit your Italian soda out—go for it! Remember, if you laugh at each thing he says you have nowhere to go from there but down. I made that mistake with a guy who was hilarious; funny stories, physical comedy, the whole nine feet. Problem was as soon as he started to run out of jokes he got a little nervous and tried to be funnier and funnier. He would go out of his way to make me laugh, but before long the magic had worn off and I felt like beating him about the upper body with an extinguisher every time he opened his fat, humorless face. If he wasn't being funny he had nothing to say. *Yuck!* Laugh when it's funny, but only when it's sincere.

Talk About Past Boyfriends: Woo . . . quick snore! Look out! Do you want to hear about Peggy the tennis star and her perky breasts? No? Then do you think he wants to hear about Derek the child actor or Les the drummer with multiple personalities? Those stories are just *made* for girls' night with the Ben and Jerry's, *Scream* on the VCR, and a venetian mud mask. If you get too entwined in your past heartaches he may think a) you are a heifer to be feared and avoided at all costs or b) a really mean filly who will only bad-mouth anyone who takes her to the rodeo. This is a sin I didn't commit when I was younger because I didn't really have past boyfriends to speak of since I rarely made it past the first friggin' date! Be nice, talk about the two of you. There is a lot less intrigue in your romantic past than you might think.

Give It Up: I realize the temptation is so strong to rip off your sarong and slather up in each other's sweat and DNA, but first-date inter-course historically becomes a one-night stand, which is usually not the desired effect when you like someone. It doesn't matter how old you are, how inexperienced, how many times you've been married. I *know* it's easy to lose your good sense when a date, especially a first one, has gone off extraordinarily well. I know so many buttoned-up young women who give up the goods in fits of irrational ecstasy only to regret it the next day or ten minutes after. If you really, really like a boy and want to be his lingering love then wait until the appropriate time to

121

Me and Mickey, Junior Class President and my prom date. I didn't get a kiss.

charm the pants off him. If you do it too soon he'll think you are kind of loosey-goosey and he won't invite you to that Halloween chowder cook-off all the cute couples go to. There is a time and place for everything.

Panic: Don't panic! Did you stain his Dockers with tomato juice? No problem! Pat the stain with a napkin soaked with club soda. Did you call him the wrong name? Forget about it! Keep calling him different names until it becomes a joke. Conversation stalled? Whatever! Run, don't walk to a movie theater. View the film, then chat over decaf ☕ (no need to wind yourself up anymore with that pesky caffeine). There is basically nothing on a date that is worth panicking over. Always take a quarter for emergency phone calls, always have a way out and a ride home, and never get yourself locked in a car with a drunk, horny boy. It would be a shame to have to castrate a boy on a first date. If you don't put yourself in dumb situations in the first place there is less reason to panic.

Dates are like snowflakes, no two are alike and they can be either beautiful or just plain cold. There are so many ways to approach dates, hopefully a list of things *not* to do can help you out in a pinch. I still get nervous when my man takes me out on a date. I guess that's the nature of sticking your tongue out in a snowstorm.

122

Questionable

What If He Has a Cold Sore? *Oooooooohhh!* Yuck! A cold sore is as bad as a prison record! You're not born with either and they are impossible to get rid of. I know it's politically correct to have sympathy for every freak under the sun, but cold sores? That's where I draw the line, and if cleanliness or a couth appearance is important to you I think you'd better do the same . . . *Draw that line, tighten your lips, sister!* Do you think Nicole Kidman and Tom Cruise smooched with open wounds? Never! You can go your whole life without contracting a cold sore as long as you don't kiss boys with open sores on their faces or share drinks with people who admit to having had a cold sore (that includes sharing lip balm), and for goodness' sake use some discretion when swapping bodily fluids.

Should I Sneak Out to See Him? Oh, I remember this one . . . I had a friend whose house I'd stay at and we would sleep on the front lawn. It was kind of like camping only without the bugs, desolation, kerosene stove, tent, and wilderness. We did have some wild animals come visit

123

every once in a while, if you know what I mean (wink-wink). Woo-hoo! Teenage lust monkeys, here I come! It wasn't as risky as going to some love shack miles away. If anything really went wrong we could just scream and the neighbors would run out in their boxer shorts and save us. But really, it's much more fun to sneak out with girls than with boys. If you go out to see him in the middle of the night he may be expecting the mamba when all you want to do is the waltz. You catch my drift? Plus, if you are in a car in the middle of the night local authorities tend to frown on fraternizing on their turf and they'll be happy to arrest you. It's happened to quite a few of my friends, not to mention Mary K. Letourneau and her preteen stealth master. You get comfortable in the back of the Saturn, you mildly disrobe, and all of a sudden . . . *bam!* 🚔 sirens, lights, a criminal record, your mother's in tears, and you can forget about the llama for your birthday. You'll be in the hangar . . . grounded. No, don't sneak out to see him. If you must have an après-bedtime rendezvous (it all sounds so romantic!) have him come to you, to your bedroom window if it's on the ground floor. That way the situation is all in your control, he's on your territory and you can smooch in the night air and go back to sleep.

Should I DO It? If you have to ask then probably not. As previously stated, this is something that has a no return policy, no exceptions, no exchanges. I don't have too many friends who sit around and go "Man, if only I'd done it sooner with that guy I wasn't very serious about who pressured me so hard. I think my life would have been more complete." You will never know how good it feels to wait unless you, well . . . wait! I have so many friends that gave it up for the wrong reasons, pressure from him, pressure from friends, spontaneity. You know what

124

a better activity is? A vacation! At least you'll have pictures and if you decide you hate it you can leave early and never go there again. If you do it too soon you have no pictures (please, *God!),* you risk teenage pregnancy, a damaged reputation, and disease. About that reputation, once it's gone it's hard to retrieve. I've heard of doctors performing radical hymen replacement, but trying to reinstate a good reputation once a lady has been labeled a tart? Quite impossible!

What If I Am Ready? Then make absolute sure he is trustworthy, responsible, and disease free. Make him get an HIV test and look at the results with your own eyes. And don't even *think* about playing doctor without contraception. There have been miraculous breakthroughs in condom technology recently including thinner condoms, polyurethane for users with latex sensitivity, colors, sparkles, ribbing, spermicidal (nonoxynol-9 is highly recommended if your body can tolerate it), and a plethora of others. Remember, responsibility is a huge turn-on. Buy, unwrap, and properly use that birth and disease control device. You can ask a doctor, nurse, or knowledgeable adult about other complementary forms of BC including sponges, diaphragms, pills, female condoms, spermicidal mousse and gel, and a few others. If you are not mature enough to provide your own birth control then for goodness' sake you are not ready to have sex. When it comes time to actually do it if you don't feel right then don't do it. It's not like going to the movies where once you buy the ticket and popcorn you are obligated to sit down and see the whole show.

Should I Let Him Suck on My Toes? Hmmmmmmmm . . . an interesting one. This has more to do with the relationship you have with your own feet. *Do* you have singing, pride-inducing pigs that really need introduction into another's mouth? If that's the case then who am I to hold you back? Some people get off doing the darndest things, and foot love is a very common, harmless fetish. I once had a cab driver in New York beg me to take off my shoes so he could give me a rubdown. Don't bother yourself with the visualization, I didn't give in. I would rather have walked into a beehive covered in pollen and powdered sugar, and I hate bees! Feet are very personal, very naughty. If he's asking and you are a free spirit then by all means indulge. Wear pretty, festive polish and toe rings, and remember that feet are a good place for first tattoos as well.

Does It Feel Good to Get Felt Up? Not if you are self-conscious about your boobs and don't trust the guy. If you're sitting there thinking, "Ohmygod, he hates my body, he can feel my ribs, I smell, oh lord, he thinks my nipples feel weird, good gravy, he probably thinks I'm a slut for letting him do this, I probably kiss bad, oh my garden, why did I just grunt, I sounded like a pig . . ." then it will eventually wear down the fun. But if you are really excited and confident it is a turn-on and everyone benefits. As far as being felt up goes, just relax and let your mind shut up for a little bit. Once you let your body take over you will enjoy everything a whole lot more. But don't do anything too soon. If you are having any questions about whether or not it's the right time, then it's too soon, so wait.

What If He Can't Kiss Very Well? This is a mortal sin and on its own enough to spit on the fiery passion that is young love. Each lover needs to know the fine, fine art of kissing. It is so delicate and important. The lips need to be pouty and supple, naughty yet chaste. The tongues need to intertwine at different rhythms in order to convey the particular moment whether it be heated cramping lust or soft rose petal romance. Your main man needs to read whether you need a gentle slow peck and embrace or a good wet slathering involving all the glands—salivary, pituitary, lymph—simultaneously. You need to be able to kiss a man with your eyes and fingers, he needs to be slapped when you walk away just by the gentle swaying of your hips. If he is new to kissing then enlighten him if you feel he's worthy, direct him with your soul, teach him with your tongue, be French. If he is simply limp-lipped, uninspired, or has bad breath then drop him immediately, make up some excuse, and seek out the contestant behind door number two. It is a shame to be a bad kisser, it is so telling of an empty soul. You deserve better. You deserve a great kiss.

Should I Touch It? That's a tricky one. Once you've committed to handling the merchandise it's very difficult to go back to browsing around the store. It's best to think with your head and not your hand in this situation, but if you have put off sexual activity for months and you really feel he needs a womanly release then this is the best means to go about getting the job done. Remember, he is an expert in snake handling so you have to be careful not to harm or embarrass him. If he gives you advice take it. If he complains it's not enough tell him tough. Men have survived for years with a lot less action so if you are willing to shake the bacon he better be thankful. Make sure you know he's worthy, once again, before you give manual love. It can be a sticky situation.

Should I Kiss It? Probably not, unless you are of enough age and maturity that you can look him in the eye at a party after performing such an act without feeling really stupid (this is another good litmus test). Remember that oral offerings are just as unsanitary as unprotected sex. You can perform this more safely by employing your friend the flavored condom but they actually taste like balloons and don't do much for the old integrity. You can get freaky and nasty in more creative ways that won't leave the boys chuckling and comparing you to the Big Lewinsky. There is so little intrigue in a young woman who gives blow jobs too freely, it's such a cliché. Prudes are much more fascinating, especially if they wear garters.

What If He's Too Hairy? You aren't going to get everything you want in one boy, so you have to weigh what you've got, what's most important to you, and what you absolutely cannot live with. Does he have beautiful brown eyes, saucers of chocolate milk that make you wanna slurp? Does he hold your hand in public? Does he have a cute laugh and strong arms? If he does then you can probably live with a little back hair. I know it's kind of gross, but think what you're giving up! This is not your early thirties so you can still break up with boys over relatively minor quirks, but if you really enjoy the majority of his person then maybe it's best to live with a little flaw. The little things always drove me up a wall about guys after the first week's lust grip wore off. I once became repulsed by a guy because he had a big mouth full of pizza and he laughed super hard. The visual wouldn't leave me, especially when I went to kiss him good night. If you're being picky just for the sake of finding someone perfect you might as well give up, because you will never, ever find perfection. If you suddenly become incensed by everything he does then it may be time to call it quits and trust your instincts. That female intuition is as handy in matters of the heart as butter in a pastry kitchen, it's just not as fattening. Plus, there's always Nair and waxing.

What If He Doesn't Take No for an Answer? Anytime you get yourself in a confined space with a guy you don't know make sure you have a way out in case things go wrong. You can be having a perfectly pleasant time rolling around during an innocent grope when he goes too far and asks for some sweet treat you're not willing to give him. I have been in a few situations where the other half of a teenage romp feels the contract of lip lock includes aggressive sexuality. When I refused one guy tried to pin me down. I was lucky enough to push him off me and hop out of the car so he could calm down for a little bit as I threatened to kill him. Never, *ever* give in to someone's demands if they go beyond your comfort level. Don't put yourself in a situation where you can't get out or you can't fight because you're too drunk or high. Most important, *get out of there* as soon as you sense his desire and good sense are going south. It's better to have a close call and have him hate you than to be violated and hate yourself. No is no is no is no.

How Can I Defend Myself? If it does turn awful out of the blue, there are a few things you can do. The first is to obviously get out of there immediately and avoid any further physical confrontation. The second is to use your voice and startle him. Say, "Hey! What do you think you're doing? Get off of me right now, jackass, or you're going to be in serious trouble!" Be very authoritative so he knows you mean *no*. If he does attack you his most sensitive area is his groin so kick or punch

129

him in the sack as hard as you possibly can and exit as he's writhing in pain. Never do this to a guy as a joke. It hurts a lot worse than getting elbowed in the boob during PMS. Males have more upper-body strength than females so don't try to get in a hitting match. Get on the floor and kick the daylights out of him. Scratch him or poke him in the eyes 👁, grab some big object and hit him and keep screaming the whole time. Eighty-five percent of rapes occur between two people who know each other as acquaintances, relatives, or dates. Don't let the fact that you know your attacker stop you from going to the police immediately. Call a friend ☎ and have them come get you or meet you but don't wait to get help. You don't want these losers to become repeat offenders. Sexual assault has to end and in order for the chain to be broken the abusers need to be brought down. If you do get abused it's not your fault, just tell someone and get help right away.

OnLy thE Lonely

I think the loneliest time I can recall growing up, other than the year I
spent as an urchin on that Bolivian cruise ship, was my freshman year
in high school when I was plagued by some mystery virus that kept me
out of school half the year. Since our school was structured like a
squash tournament with several round-robin layers of bitchy cliques,
it was hard to get involved in any one peer group if you weren't around
to keep up. My main junior high rocker gang, lovingly dubbed "The
Peons" by my older brother Brian (thanks Bri), had disbanded and we
went our separate ways in the overwhelming rush and excitement of
high school. I had KiKi to hang out with but she was grounded so much
we hardly saw each other outside of school. I can't tell you the agony
of sitting home alone on Friday and Saturday nights thumbing through
my sparse phone book looking for some action as I watched my two
older brothers pile themselves into packed cars with their loud music
 and loose girlfriends. I would settle for watching dumb movies with
my parents but somehow *Dirty Dancing* the third time around seemed
like miserable socializing for any fourteen-year-old. I had to act. With-

131

out any constant group involvement your name was left off party lists and your phone stayed silent. I sure liked a lot of individuals at school, but to be included in the weekend action you had to be tight. I was sad. KiKi and I didn't have cars and her parents already had her for the next four weekends due to some lame "gambling ring" she'd supposedly started between first and second periods. What could I possibly do? What you should do if you're bummed and lonely and gamy and hostile. Everything! I marched around school and signed up for every imaginable extracurricular activity . . . well, none of the dork ones like Mathletes or Drill Team. I joined the Service Club, the Croquet Society, Youth Legislature, Saferide because—hey!—people needed rides home on the weekends when they were drunk. It was an instant excuse. It turned out a lot of the people I got to know weren't caught up in the goofy hierarchy of dorks and jocks, they were just trying to beef up their college applications with some well-rounded, wholesome activity. After a few short weeks I started talking to a whole new batch of people I'd never considered hanging out with at school. When I saw some of my Croquet friends or someone I'd volunteered with blowing up balloons for a marathon we immediately had something to joke about, or at least acknowledge each other for. Even the slightest head nod from someone

Me at age fourteen with my Service Club buddies Neil, Alex, and Geoff. They're still my friends today!

was an accomplishment for me in a way, it chipped away at my loneliness.

The best way to combat boredom, I found that year, is to find something to do. Because I was sick I wasn't attending classes regularly and when I was well I was skipping them like a scratched forty-five, but hey! I was finally swinging! Because I was so involved I looked like a do-gooder to my parents and the school faculty and I got to meet one of my very best friends, Geoff, through the Service Club. The Service Club was a philanthropic service organization he started to aid the poor and dehydrated. Geoff was the most brilliant person in school and one of those seniors you think is way too important and unattainable as a friend. I think he felt kind of bad for me so he started hanging out with me on the weekends, including me in trash collecting retreats and making sure I wasn't spending my idle time doing anything illegal. My mom liked him so much that after he graduated from high school she would fly me down to Stanford once a year so his genius would rub off on me, no pun intended. It didn't rub on anything unfortunately; I ended up attending Pasadena City College for two weeks.

I did find that genuine friendships and mutual interests are about the most positive thing going for a wayward and lonely lady. If ever you find yourself in a position of total boredom, then sniff around your school and community and find out what people are doing with themselves. Chances are you'll find the party is wherever you make it and people everywhere are looking for some productive ways to spend their Friday and Saturday nights, other than those *Dirty Dancing* film festivals that have become so popular. I became interested in things I never knew about and ended up getting motivated for the rest of my career as a Lakeridge High School Pacer, not to mention my future career as a professional croquet ingenue and part-time trash collector. If you do join some of these organizations stay away from the Mathletes. You don't get a varsity letter and they have been known to run a few prostitution rings. You didn't hear that from me. A Service Club member would *never* spread that kind of filth.

So YOu waNNA
Be a Nun

Think about what your life is like now: You flip on the TV and casually watch the news or *The Simpsons*, you ride around on your bike or talk on the phone. Imagine now that you had given it all up for a higher calling ✢ where your schedule was rigorously dictated and you placed all your faith in God. I had the opportunity to speak with a young Orthodox nun who tells what it's really like to give up a life of materialism for devoted spirituality and live as a monastic.

OK, from this point on I won't use your name. Great! That is great. **So is it OK to say that you are an Orthodox nun?** Yes. **Our interview will stick to just straight question and answer.** Okay, because when you speak with us, we don't have a blessing to speak about personal things. I can speak to you about general things, but, like, my personal things that personally concern me, I will not be able to answer you. **May I ask you how you decided to become a nun?** Oh, that is the first question that you can't ask. **OK.** What I can say to you is it is a call. They use that word "calling" and basically, it is. It is from God. Depending on the person, it all depends on each person. There is not one general answer for everybody. **Was there ever a time when you wanted to be a layperson and get another job, or did you always feel like you have been a nun?** For most of us here, we have not been here too long. We were out in the world. We were in school. God can enlighten someone, like a spiritual father, and through

Me, KiKi, and Kari, practicing to be nuns.

that someone can decide that what the world is offering is not exactly what they want. The world, right now, it is obviously too material for many people. I guess for everybody. But for a person who decides to become a monastic, it is to the point where they choose to be with God, they want to live in Christ, for Christ, and just forget about the world. And that is why it is kind of hard for me to answer questions pertaining to the world, because it is something that we want to forget. Not that we have anything against the people in the world, but for our personal salvation. **How long does it take to become a nun?** Well, when someone decides to come to the monastery, you are going through a trial period. You are called a novice. But as soon as you come to the monastery you are considered a monastic. You can be a novice for two years, you can be a novice for five years. It is a personal thing. It also depends on your spiritual father, your elder, which is Father Efrem. He is the one who has established these monasteries in the United States and in Canada. He was an ascetic for fifteen years in the desert on Mount Athos during the fifties and the sixties. He is a wonderful person. **What kind of experiences did he go through as an ascetic?** Basically, he lived a life where he did not have any connection with the world. Out in the middle of nowhere where there is nothing. What he had to eat was whatever was growing in the desert. He is also the elder at one of the big monasteries on Mount Athos right now. There are ten right now in North America and he is establishing more. Well, anyway, my point is that Father Efrem is basically establishing these monasteries in North America because there is a cry for Christ. People are not satisfied with what is out there. They are longing for Christ. **What happens after one's novice period?** It is like a tonsuring. That is where you are given another name. You are sure that you are going to stay in the monastery. Once a person has come here and is in that novice stage, it is kind of like a trial stage. You are here, but you don't know if you are here for good. Once you are tonsured a nun, it is almost a certainty that you are going to be here. **Is it fun doing what you do? Do the sisters have fun together?** Oh, sure. But it is hard. It's not easy, it is not easy. **Is it hard to become a nun?** It is not a difficult process, it is just not too easy to be able to. It is just that you know that God is with you and you know that he is covering you. It is not a very easy thing to be here every day once, let's say, you are used to having your own will and going wherever you want. **Are there ever times when you guys get sad because there are things you want to do outside and there are things that you want to do of your own free will a little bit more?** Sure. Those are the temptations that one goes through. It is part of it. It is part of being a Christian as well. But like I said, for any Christian as well, you have to take your cross and follow Christ. But it

137

is out of your own free will that you decided to give up your will. **What is a typical day like for you?** We get up at two o'clock, that is when we do our individual prayer, we do our prayer robes and have prostrations that we do every night. After supplication, which finishes at five-thirty, you are free to sleep. We don't exceed seven hours [of sleep] a day. We have breakfast at eight. Then we have a lot of crafts. We make a lot of decorated icons with flowers. There is a sister that paints flowers, but we also have the traditional Byzantine icons. They are laminated. We also do iconography. There is also embroidery, the traditional embroidery that they do. At five o'clock we get together and have supplications in church. Three times a week we have divine liturgy. We go to sleep around nine-thirty or ten depending on the person. And we are up at two again. We are very busy. **Do the sisters still see their families?** Sure, families visit. Some families live farther than others, but sure they do. **Do you ever travel?** We have visited other monasteries when they have their feast days. **If you wanted to see a museum in some other country, would you be allowed to do that?** No, I don't think so. Then again, there are certain things, it all depends on the reason. **Do you ever get to eat special things like chocolate?** Sure. There are certain things we don't eat. We don't eat meat. We don't ever eat meat. **Oh, neither do I. I don't like the taste of chicken.** Wow! See, that is your decision out of your own will, right? **How do you stay so calm?** Well, as a monastic, whatever we do during the day, our mind is constantly on prayer. So we try to be praying at all times. We say the Jesus prayer, I don't know if you are familiar with the prayer "Lord Jesus Christ, have mercy on me"? **Do you get books and newspapers?** Our abbess does. She gets books and she is quite informed and if there is anything she believes needs to be given to us, she will. As for nuns, we are not exposed to anything out there. **How do you get to**

138

be an abbess? An abbess? I guess with a lot of virtues. **Are you in your twenties?** Yes. **What advice can you give to a young girl who is tempted to do things that maybe she shouldn't?** That is a hard question. They are faced with a lot of pressures in school and in society as a whole. They have to become their own person, but no matter what they do, no matter where they go, they have to know in their hearts, they have to believe that there is a God out there. They have to believe that there is something. Everything is so materialistic. If you have God in your life things are different. It is OK for them to love God. They shouldn't be ashamed of what they believe in or what they have been brought up in. That is easier said than done, but it is also good to let them know we exist. We are not your typically dressed sixty-to-seventy-year-old nuns. You know we are young, just like they are. And it is OK to decide to give up everything for Christ because you are just looking for your salvation, for God I should say. **Thank you, Sister.**

InTErnEt Love

I'd never want to fall in love ♡ with a guy I met on the Internet. The feelings are not real, the connection may be insincere. There is a false notion that falling in love with someone's words on the computer screen is much purer than falling in love with their looks. What you are doing is falling for an illusion. Can you really be yourself online? Isn't it all too easy to formulate the perfect persona and Teflon phrases without the spontaneous reaction only physical contact can bring? Think about it, you may be falling for a perfect picture in your head that is a frightening fabrication, a whimsied farce some geology professor has dreamed up between lectures. Anyone can sound dreamy on a computer screen. I'm sure my uncles can sound more beautiful than Brad, Leo, and Lou Ferrigno combined, but . . . eeeewwwww!

    I liked a boy over the phone but he turned out to be dumb and fat and had gross hair and was a compulsive liar. Do you think that blossoming romance ended in marriage? Try a restraining order. It goes like this . . . you're curious and bored (a lethal combination for a teenager) and begin browsing chat rooms like they are Banana Republic storefronts, only this time you have a platinum card with a $600,000 limit in an empty mall on a three-day weekend. You know you wish you looked a little different so you embellish about your hourglass shape, glossy nails, wheat-blond hair, whole milk complexion, new Lexus, scholarship to Oxford . . . yadada, skudiddlydopalopadada (I think I knew a nice Greek kid with that last name) and *wham!* You have yourself a new identity. There is nothing wrong with harmless embellishments and exploration but when you and Norbert the computer programmer from Boise who has posed as Porter the national water polo champion and underwear model begin making plans for a six-day rendezvous in Guadalajara that's when you have to put a halt on the ovary bus and pull yourself up by the knee-highs. Is this what you really want? An assumed love with someone whose hobbies may include popping his backne in the mirror, genital baths from PuffPuff the longhaired Siamese cat, and fooling young women into believing he is a future Olympian? Someone who disgraces the good name of water polo? Good heavens, have some self-respect. How do you think he's going to feel when he sees you're not really the 5′ 11″, 104-pound Croatian supermodel you built yourself up to be? It's hard finding real love in a world with so many laptops, it's harder when everyone else is so deceptive. You don't know you're attracted to someone until you feel your pheromones mingle, until your hands and fingers interlock and brush one another in a handshake, or at least until you've heard their voice or seen their eyes. I'm not naming names but a very good friend of mine met a guy on the phone, became obsessed with his voice and his practiced false perfection, fell for him madly, and believed him when he said he was infertile. Needless to say they manufactured a child when their fluids intermixed and she raises the healthy young'n six years later (without the help of his father, of course).

It's so easy to get infatuated, especially when your heart has been longing for a buddy for so long without results. It's so easy to fall into the trap of: "But he really loves me . . . for me!" He is infatuated with an idea and ideas are the worst boyfriends and girlfriends of all. Be wise, use that frisky modem for experimentation, have a mad technological lark in the computer lab in the library. Just don't let the ticker skip away with fantastic notions of meeting Mr. HonestyIntegrityHot-Pants online. Maybe you'll meet in line for tickets to the boat and rifle show, or at the driving range, the mall, the taxidermist, but not the computer. Boys are a lot more fun in person.

143

tHE Sound anD The Fury oF Music

Taste in music  is an entirely personal thing. People often underestimate the importance of music: parents scoff at the sound of the bass beating from behind their teenager's door, teachers ridicule the lyrics of the songs their students listen to. But along with things like your siblings and geographic location, music is paramount in sculpting your environment and your identity. It provides a key to understanding your world.

It's hard to find music that you really love. First, you are constantly bombarded with popular music and without other options you are led to believe that's all there is. For a sad section of society Top 40 is as far as they stray into the musical jungle, and we know those rations can be dumbed-down vanilla, simple offerings that hardly deserve a second listen let alone the billions we spend on them. Second, building an arsenal of great music is time-consuming and really, really expensive. Some bands go out of their way to keep album prices low so people on every rung of the ladder can afford to experience them.

These saints are few and far between and should be rewarded with re-spect and dancing and tattoos all over your body in the drummer's 🥁 likeness. Everyone else charges an arm and a leg, so younger fans are left to skim used bins, tape off 📼 their friends, or settle for buying a few key things a year. I wish I had much more time to memorize CD's and peruse the aisles of good record stores. It's so excellent when you go to a store that carries great, hard-to-find music. Especially when the people who work there are open to giving you suggestions and don't act condescending if you haven't heard of the band they're

Me and Anthony Kiedis at the Video Music Awards.

recommending. I love this one guy in a record store in Seattle. Each time we go in we leave with five or six CD's because he gets so enthu-siastic about so many different bands. It's as if he lives to turn people on to music they've never heard. If you can find a few good, nice men-tors like this they will help you morph into the kind of music collector one could only dream of. Find someone who will broaden your mind.

It's very easy to get stuck in a style rut, just like it's easy to get stuck wearing black or brown for years at a time. Once in a while you need to throw in a red scarf or blue bonnet. My male companion has a habit of rolling his eyes whenever I pick up a Willie Nelson record. Sometimes I feel like the Red-Headed Stranger. I used to go into stores and look for the same style of music, same beat, same types of bands, same safe boundaries. I was literally frightened to try other styles as if somehow I needed to be fluent in each language and not knowing about them was reason enough not to go near them. I didn't realize how important it was to really sample until one man, one huge music fan, changed my tastes and the way my CD player grooves forever.

It was a sultry July in New York. Eggs were frying on the side-walk, hipsters were floating above the street balancing on a wave of cool. Happiness rocked out of every piss-filled crack, watermelon was for sale. It was a magical New York summer night and my friend Hank decided to take me shoppin'. I had met Henry Rollins seven years earlier when I was interning at KROQ. He is a hulk of a guy, all hard knotted muscle, tense jaw, tattoo; a real eye-catcher. He is the former lead singer of Black Flag and currently tours the world with his band The Rollins Band, owns a publishing company for music and books, and is an overall societal sounding board willing to take on any subject. His spoken word performances last up to two and a half hours and, although it sounds like a little bit of a cliché, he can make you laugh and cry within the course of an evening. He likes to make fun of me on-stage once in a while, but I get even by making fun of him in person. Dinner with Hank is like a private spoken word performance because he goes on and on from tale to tale until he gets tired and leaves to write in his daily journal. I'm convinced he goes home and has phone sex with college cheerleaders, or at least visits their Web sites.

On such a night, as I was saying, Hank and I got talking about jazz. I should say Hank talked about jazz for two hours. I sat there ignorant and dumbfounded as he rattled off at least a hundred CD's and artists, each of which, he claimed, "changed my life," or, was "the greatest record ever made." At the top of his list was none other than the train, John Coltrane, arguably the greatest American musician to have ever lived. I nodded deceptively as Henry demanded, "You know Coltrane, right?" "Oh yeah, sure," I said. No, I was kind of a lost lamb. I'd heard the name but never the music. He marched me into the record store, plunked down $9.95, and bought me one of the greatest records I've ever heard, *A Love Supreme*. It was Coltrane's album for God, a great man's greatest work written as a thank you to the man upstairs. Now, Hank has lost more records than I will ever own in my life and he spends hours each day listening intently to jazz, Latin, and all other types of music. It is the thing that lubes his chassis, turns his rudder, jiggles his handle. I love music and have been gainfully employed by it for some years but had it not been for that hot night I don't know if my tastes would have budged in this decade of my life. I was stale. Now every time I hear John Coltrane, or any jazz for that matter, my legs and feet tap and jitter and I think of Hank lifting five hundred pounds in free weights off his chest humming the same bars. I love to fly out of my chair when I hear Ella Fitzgerald, I love to shake my melon back and forth to Chet Baker and Stan Getz. I wouldn't have done that without someone to kindly and patiently open my horizons and pry my music chest open enough to let a little light in. The sooner you can find someone to help you find new music, whether it's an older brother or sister, your hip parents (as rare as the Hope Diamond, I'm afraid), or the guy with the big lamb chops at the music store, the better off you'll be.

Not everyone gravitates to the same kind of music. This is not a matter of exposure and will, it is a scientific fact. Have you ever watched a baby boogie when a certain song comes on the radio or jiggle her baby fat when the opening theme of *Sesame Street* plays? We have deep within us a biological pitch pipe that has a natural vibration and predisposition. Granted, what you are raised on will have a drastic impact on what you will listen to for a time, but if you pay attention to how your body responds ♫ you'll find a lot of what you like has been there from the beginning. Some people are sickened by the sounds of country music, physically made ill by the likes of Trisha Yearwood and Willie Nelson. Other people will die unless they are regularly injected with salsa and samba. Do you find yourself dry-heaving listening to The Carpenters in Muzak on a long elevator ride? Try this, it's an experiment. For one calendar year I want you to open your CD player to every type of music you can imagine. Stop setting limits for yourself based on what your friends find acceptable. Give a spin to Johnny Cash the Man in Black, try Miles Davis on for size, listen to the Clash or old Michael Jackson, anything you have either been opposed to or kept from in the past. This is what the best musicians have done their whole lives. Maybe you'll become a famous accordion player after the epiphany you'll get from a polka record. The sooner you let your guard down the happier you'll be because you will really experience music instead of just going along with what you think other people want. It is impossible to be hip anymore, not to mention expensive and time-consuming to try to be. You'll never please everyone! Not with your clothes or your makeup or the color of your skin and especially not your music. Don't be ashamed to sneak in those guilty pleasures before bedtime. Go ahead and play that Hanson or Menudo record you've been hiding from your friends, but be sure you temper the pop with classical, jazz, blues, or anything else you consider elevator music. Instead of waiting for your favorite music to be played why not learn to appreciate every style of music, so the next time you are at a dance or wedding each song that's played will be your favorite.

tHe

International Language

"Oh, I wish I was an Oscar Mayer wiener , eating wieners speaking Japanese, or even blabbing Spanish or Italian to better my job opportunities."

This could be your mantra! There is a cult of mathematicians who believe fervently that algebra and her notorious relatives are the only saviors of soul, conscience, and humanity. These people are lucky if they have a stamp from Canada in their passports, and if they do it's usually from one of the English-speaking provinces. I remember the ridiculous speeches these antisocialites used to spout every time someone complained about boring tests and monotonous homework assignments: ". . . math is everything and everywhere, the music we listen to, the food we eat is all mathematically measured . . . numbers are all . . . stand and praise integers, fractions, and derivatives . . . without math you are a zero . . ." Blah. Blah. Blah.

When I was fifteen and in the midst of algebraic hell I decided to phone one of my better-educated associates who had found high school repugnant and boring. He thought the whole damn experience was a

151

waste of time that kept him away from his "real" education. Intrigued by his frequent tirades, I asked him what I could really learn while I was still in high school, what subjects could further my chances for success in the "real world." He thought hard and silently and came up with a subject I had completely taken for granted—foreign languages. Sharing my consummate disdain for all things numerical, he said French and Spanish classes were his only well-spent time during his four years in the pasty white stucco of our secondary educational facility. I'm sure you have teachers who tell you this kind of stuff all the time and it may sound like a well-rehearsed load of reworked dog biscuits, but the truth of the matter is bilingualism is an impressive and worthwhile pursuit that gives you enormous social, personal, and professional advantages. Do you realize how many countries speak French? Do you know how many friends you could make if you knew more Spanish than *"Yo quiero Taco Bell"*?

I got to interview Eric Bergoust, gold medalist in men's aerials, at the Winter Olympics in Nagano. (Peter Myers)

The greatest foreign policy maker in the latter half of this century knew as many as fifteen languages. That person's name is Richard Milhous Nixon, God rest his soul. I hear his Latin could put the pope to shame. Because of his thoughtful and selfless forays into the world of foreign policy a lot of Americans have been able to take boarders and cultures for granted. When I was in Nagano, Japan, covering the XVIII Olympic Winter Games for CBS I saw the most beautiful sight— Japanese children singing in the falling snow outside a centuries-old sacred temple. My co-worker and I were nearly in tears over our Filet-O-Fishes at the McDonald's by the hotel. The Japanese were so amazingly hospitable that they had erected a special McDonald's 🍔 in the broadcast center. They truly went out of their way to make us feel at home thousands of miles across the Pacific. Do you know how many of us repaid them? We pushed them around, snapped at shop owners when we had to wait in lines, and took advantage of lax scalping laws by hoarding and selling tickets to events at ridiculous prices. *And all in English!!!!* When we did take the time and courtesy to use a Japanese phrase in a soft voice the people there were so pleased, although they did get a good laugh when we mispronounced things. At dinner, one of the CBS producers meant to thank a sushi chef for the delectable fish. Instead he announced to the whole restaurant that he had a morning erection. But at least the chef seemed to appreciate the effort.

There's no question but that it is hard to stumble through a foreign language when you travel abroad. The first time you venture outside of England, Australia, or some other English-speaking land it is quite a shock trying to hold a coherent conversation. I remember trying to order Chinese take-out 🥡 in Paris a few years ago from a woman who spoke no English. I was so humiliated and frustrated because I couldn't understand a thing she was trying to say to me. It's easy enough to gather a few key phrases when you travel, but unless someone physically points to where you need to go it is nearly impossible to grasp the information at the seemingly warp speed at which the natives speak. *Ou est la banque?* It sounds harmless, but what if the answer is go six blocks down, take a quick right, then cut behind the jail next to the nuclear power plant. Could you get all that? In French? I just used my credit card and traveler's checks, thank you.

It is no surprise that people from all over the world are finding their home in the United States at the same time that so many businesses are looking to hire assertive, well-versed bilingual men and women. People need to communicate and it's silly to assume they all want to do so in our language. There was a neato-bandito girl named Sunny in my senior English class who went to Thailand on an exchange program and learned the language . . . *in three months!* I met another wonderful man in Nagano named Mario who spoke seven languages fluently. We did a fun story for CBS where we went to the athletes' village and welcomed a lot of the arriving athletes and lightly conversed in many languages as a gesture of goodwill, friendship, and global 🌐 ♡ love. Mario knew every way to say hello, how are you, do you like ham in your omelet, do you like my knickers. He had obviously done a lot of traveling and studying and had an uncanny ability to retain languages and information. He said it's easy, the trick to learning any language and to separate it from the others you already know is to *think in that language!* It worked for him and I dare you to try it and see if it works for you.

Next time someone insists that excelling at math is the only way to survive in our all-consuming world of technology and numerical morsels, you just tell that person to take a trip to a remote village in the Far East and see how far they get with their calculator and protractor. Don't get me wrong, math is extremely useful and has its

154

place—if you like it, by all means go ahead and study it. But also further your education and your communication by learning new languages. They'll help you expand your cultural horizons, get yourself out of disastrous situations, and better the reputations of Americans everywhere. Oh, by the way, the best Filet-O-Fish I've *ever* had was in Japan. *Domo arigato!*

oNE on OnE
wiTh *Jamila Wideman*

I read an article about Jamila Wideman a few years ago in *Sports Il-lustrated* and was incredibly struck by her poise and honesty. As the backbone of the Stanford University women's basketball program she dominated women's basketball and electrified the game, helping it gain the immense popularity it enjoys today as a professional sport. Jamila is now a point guard for the Los Angeles Sparks and is an ideal spokesperson for her team, her league, and women everywhere who have embraced athleticism as a form of expression and sanctity. People like Jamila teach us so much through their actions and words. She exemplifies many of the reasons why participation in sports is vital for young women. Whether you're shooting for the WNBA or running a few times a week to stay in shape, Jamila's words and wisdom will have an impact on how you see yourself, sports, and being active in general.

How long have you been in the WNBA? This is my second year. **How do you like it so far?** Thus far I've had a great time. It was actually a really strange transition for me coming out of college because I am basically doing all the same things I did for four years in college and now they're handing me a check for it. **How is that?** Ya know, the first couple times I kinda felt bad, like they'd give me my check and I'd kind of like slink off to the side like I was stealing something. But as I have been more involved with what I call the more businesslike aspects of being a professional player, it kinda feels more like a job. **How are the other players? How do they compare?** It was definitely a big jump, I think, for me. The best way to describe it is in college you played a good team that had one or two great players, in the WNBA you step out and all five of those players were the great player. There is not a weak link out there. **Why did you start playing basketball?** I started out because I wanted to be like my older brothers, who both played, and like my dad. So, I started out just following them to the gym Saturday mornings and I would kinda stand off to the side and dribble the ball for three hours. And eventually I got big enough so that my dad would let me play with them two on two every once in a while. **How do you think your life would be different if you had given it up?** Wow, you know, basketball, for me, has been more than just something to do. I think that being an athlete and being involved, especially in a team sport, has shaped most of my identity in that most of my best friends are people I have met through my teams or through my traveling and playing. I think I have experienced what it takes to be in a group and to go through success and joy but also to go through failure and to learn how to continue to communicate with people. And find a way to make things work. And that has become a part of how I relate to people in other areas of my life. **That transcends basketball, it must.** Oh, definitely. I think what people who have never been on a team don't realize is that most of what happens out on the floor is not necessarily a reflection of how talented or skilled the play-ers are, but instead, how well the team gets along. That definitely starts off the court. **What advice would you give to a girl who is too scared to try out for a team? She maybe thinks she has some talent, whether it is soccer, bas-ketball, lacrosse, or whatever, but she doesn't know if she is quite good enough to make it. What would you tell her?** Well, I think whatever you do whether you are trying out for a sport or anything you have to go in with some sense of confidence in yourself so that you are not swayed by the slightest failure. And I would say that going in, it would be a good idea to assume that you are going to struggle in the beginning. If you go in almost expecting that kind of adversity you are better prepared to deal with it. If you go in and expect everything to go great for the first day, that is going to happen for about 1 percent of the people who try it. The people who end up succeeding are not necessarily the ones who are best when they start out, but it's the ones who are able to come back after that really horrible first day when they were really embarrassed and maybe weren't the best out there. It is the people who go home and practice and then come back from that who usually end up being the best players or performers in the end. **How do you get that confidence in the first place?** I think there are so many things in sports you can con-trol and if you are just starting out doing something, I think one of the most important things is your approach to it, your attitude. One of the sayings my coaches used to repeat all the time is "Mental is to physi-cal as four is to one." And basically that means that you can be a less talented player but through attitude and your work ethic you can end up having as much and maybe more success as someone coming in with a lot of talent. In the same vein, in each level as you improve and move up, from your city league team to your junior high team and then

159

One on One with Jamila Wideman

high school and then college, what allows people to make that next step and to continue to improve I think is their attitude. The fact that they can come back from failure and setbacks, I mean, and there are so many examples of it. You look at athletes that were injured and were able to come back and have great careers. Michael Jordan . . . it took him eight years to win a championship. Now if after three years he had said, "Forget it. I am not good enough. I don't want to do this," then he never would have become the player that he did. **What about girls who are really, really excited about athletics when they are younger and then they are thirteen, fourteen, fifteen, and all of a sudden their bodies change and they are just getting beat down by peer pressure, what would you tell them?** It is especially hard to find a place to play, I had to play with a lot of boys. I was pretty good so the boys would respect me for my ability. There were other girls who wanted to play who hadn't necessarily played that much before and didn't get out there, because they were afraid that they weren't going to be good enough. Now, girls have to realize that even if you don't start out the best, the point of playing sports isn't necessarily that you want to become a professional basketball player. I have a lot of friends, who I played with in high school and maybe when I was younger than that, who maybe wanted to be involved, but it wasn't going to be a career and they weren't going to commit their whole life to it. There is nothing wrong with that, as long as you understand that you are playing because you enjoy it and because you have fun. You are going to get a lot of benefits out of playing that go beyond winning. That could be getting a lot of friends on your team, it is an opportunity to travel on your team, whether that is in-state, nationally, or internationally in some cases. You are learning how to work together in a group, and you are learning to communicate. Those are

160

things that, even if you stop playing after high school or when you are fifteen, are all skills and benefits that you are going to have for the rest of your life. **What is the greatest benefit for you aside from the travel and the competition, what do you get from it emotionally?** For me, it is a total confidence. A sense that this is not just something that I do, it is something that I am. And to be a part of it and to be a part of a team, I walk around with an identity that is hard for women to come by. It gives you a sense of confidence, it gives me a sense of strength in my body, physically, that I know how to take care of my body. I feel healthy and I am proud of the way I look and the things I can do. I know that I have worked very hard to be able to do those things. **How can a girl who is all about lipstick and fingernail polish and who is scared to get muddy be drawn to be an athlete? Maybe she is afraid to get sweaty or something.** It starts from a perspective that the only image of glamour or of beauty is one that has to involve makeup or dressing up. Beauty can be something other than physical appearance. The image of an athlete who is sweaty and strong is as beautiful as a woman who is 5′ 10″, 110 pounds. That, in fact, might be an unhealthy image. Have a broader perspective of what is beautiful and what it means to be feminine. Being aggressive and strong and confident are as much female characteristics as wanting to get up in the morning and blow-dry your hair and put on lipstick. **What advice would you give to a girl who just got cut from her team?** You have a choice to make right then if this is something that you want to do, that you have a passion about. And if it is, go to the coach and say, "You know what? I am going to be back next year. I really want to make this team. Give me a list of things I need to improve and can do to work on my game that would make me a player that would be attractive for your team." **Is there good competition and bad competition?** There definitely is a

One on One with Jamila Wideman

difference. Bad competition is when it is not competition anymore, it steps outside the realm of sports. If you are angry with somebody or at somebody for some reason other than what is going on out on the court then you are taking that out on them. That, to me, is no longer competition, it is pettiness and jealousy. I think competition is when two people can walk out on the court and play against each other, each wanting to win more than anything in the world, and be sweaty and get bruised and bloody, but the minute you walk across that line you can shake hands and understand that both of you were just competing. It is left on the court. **Was there ever a point where you wanted to give up? How did you keep going?** My hardest point in basketball was during my sophomore year in college, actually. I had been out for about nine months with an ankle injury and when I first came back and started playing again I really struggled physically and I struggled mentally. I had lost my confidence. I wasn't playing well. I basically did not recognize who I was out on the court anymore. And it took me almost six months to regain a sense and a strength about my ability. I remember numerous times during that stretch that I just wanted to get away and back away from it. The way I came out of it, I looked at old tapes of myself and some of the things I could do to convince myself that I had the ability and I could do it. And the other thing I did was to stop thinking so much and stop second-guessing and looking at every little thing. I remembered that the game was fun to me. What was fun was the freeness of it and the release of it. When I started thinking in those terms, and left my mind out of the play and let my body remember what it was like, that is when I think I turned it around. **Who was your greatest inspiration? Whose strength did you draw from? Was there someone like that for you?** My parents. From the athletic end of it, it was really my dad who was most involved with me on the court. He would take me and we would go shoot. He basically taught me how to play. I think as a player, one of my greatest strengths comes from my mom, determination. I am a little bit smaller than a lot of other players and a lot of people told me I was too little, I was too weak. I tried to mirror her determination and her faith in responding to people who told me that. **How tall are you?** 5′ 6″. **You are playing with women a foot taller than you and you dominate them! You rule.**

One on One with Jamila Wideman

Tina

dON't PlaY LikE thAT

Team sports, as healthy and esteem-building as they are, are not for everybody. If you are someone who has never jived in a group then check out snowboarding legend Tina Basich. For the past twelve years she has been snowboarding, designing clothing, and campaigning against breast cancer. Here's what Tina had to say when I dropped in on her.

How did you become a professional snowboarder? I started doing snowboard contests, and there was always the women's open division. **Did you ever do any team sports?** Yeah! I was pretty into team sports actually. I was really into softball and soccer. I was really into gymnastics. One day I went to gymnastics and I forgot to put my hair up so my teacher duct-taped my hair up. My mom came to pick me up and my hair was all duct-taped up and she pulled me out of it right then. That day I quit. **And how did you decide to go into such an individual sport as snowboarding?** I got into snowboarding just because it was fun. And that is still why I am doing it. The thing I like most about snowboarding that is really different than all the other sports I have competed in is that it didn't feel so competitive which made it fun. And all the girls involved and all the guys involved were always really supportive of each other. Where in gymnastics it was like glaring down your buddy before she goes on the vault kind of a thing. I think snowboarding keeps that fun,

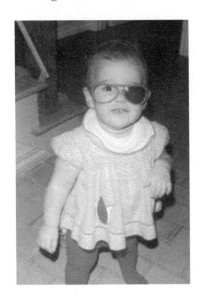

Me at eighteen months, experimenting with eyewear.

competitive, trying to push it together thing. **Do you think it is the most supportive sport as far as the women cheering each other on?** I think so from what I have seen. When I look at other sports, I see something is missing that is in snowboarding. Camaraderie. It is way easier if you are cheering your friend on rather than just trying to beat them. **How would your life be different if you had never started snowboarding?** My life would be way different if I hadn't started snowboarding. It has taught me a lot, and it has given me something that I am good at and I can be confident in. That helps out with your whole being. **Do you feel strong?** Yeah. It makes me feel strong, physically and mentally. **Do you think snowboarding is good for a girl who hates team sports?** Oh yeah! I think individual sports have a lot of confidence-building things because in individual sports you are doing it on your own. If you can feel that then you did it all on your own. **Was your family supportive of you turning pro?** My family has always been really supportive of it. Both me and my family thought it was going to be a year or two-year thing I did out of high school before I

Kennedy

went to college and it has been ten years. There never was a question of if I am doing the right thing. It is just what I wanted to do. **Is it harder to go pro in snowboarding than it is in other sports?** No, I think it is probably the easiest sport you could turn pro in. Everybody could turn pro if they wanted to. **Am I a pro because I get free One Ball Jay wax?** Oh, you're totally pro! **Who has been your biggest influence?** I think one of my all-time heroes in sports is Nadia. I could sit there and just watch her when I was younger, when I was in gymnastics. **Did you ever want to quit snowboarding and go be an accountant?** No! God, no! **What has been your best experience in this sport so far?** I think it would be meeting all the friends I have met. Even though they live all over the world. **So, every time you go somewhere you can call some of them and say, "Hey, can I stay the night?"** That is true.

Tina Don't Play Like That

Cliques

The name alone brings to mind the sound of cat  claws tapping against hard rotted flesh . . . click! Why is it chicks gravitate to other chicks in cliques only to humiliate any other chick in another clique, or worse, a chick without any clique at all? Personally, I think it is just preparing young women for the biggest cliques of all—*sororities!* Yay! Bought friends! I swear, to this day the most frightening thing to me when I'm walking through a mall (other than a demagnetized American Express) is an unruly group of teenage girls throwing daggers with their eyes and killing people with their aloof yet bitchfully aware mentality. It's not that I see myself as I was years back, although I'm sure the reason I feel the free-flowing negatrons is because I dealt them. What scares me is the fact that they are just mean. Why is this? Why are women so dead set on destroying each other in groups?

    This is not a purely adolescent phenom; nay it goes much further back. The need to humiliate and torture one another is set within our genetic code like the dormant eggs that lie in our ovaries from embryonic slumber to young adulthood. We just love to mess with each other.

Cliques start young and they often end brutally; someone's in tears with her self-esteem crumpled like a corpse in the desert waiting to audition for the Jenny Jones show later in life. Let me throw down a few examples and perhaps a few solutions to this unfortunately inherent threat.

My friend has a precocious five-year-old daughter who just started kindergarten. Do you know what her favorite thing to do is? You might think making up her own words to Barbra Streisand songs (I sure enjoy it) while simultaneously sucking on her ring and middle finger, but you'd be mistaken. She *loves* to get her two little friends together to torture and harass the weaker and less outgoing girls in the class. *At age five!!!* Why do we do this? How do we stop? But wait, there's more!

When I was in eighth grade I hung out with a pack of jackals hell-bent on making other people's lives a living heck-stain just for a cup o' laughs. One particular hideous incident I can't seem to clear from my conscience involved a sweet yet disproportionally short Southern girl whose parents moved to the Pacific NW in search of a wholesome environment for their kids (I don't care *where* you move, Ma, you get the wrong combination of estrogen carriers together and your daughter is in for a nightmare). We befriended Pequito (names have been changed to protect the abused) in such a deceptively delightful way— after-school sessions at her house, nighttime phone chats, weekend pickle binges . . . the works. Well, Pequito was a sweet girl but for us her height and naïveté were not acceptable so we dropped her like a hot pigeon in a windstorm. She tried to talk to us and become tight again but that only made it worse. Once we sensed her desperation we started to make fun of her. When she started making excuses for why she hadn't grown (she was about four feet tall) we started to grill her.

170

Oh, we'd call her names and taunt her, only to ignore her again once we got bored of it. Poor Pequito just couldn't understand *why* we were so mean to her . . . we were her friends! No, we were a clique with a far too common dynamic of search, befriend, and destroy. That's what we did! We destroyed little Pequito (is that redundant?) all for some stupid rush and mutual acceptance, we just killed her inside at a time when she should have been having the most fun . . . junior friggin' high. When she looks back on that I'm sure she winces at the time in hell she spent during her eighth-grade year, then she laughs hysterically because Pequito got the best revenge of all . . . she's now a genetic engineer finding solutions for kids all over the world who have problems with the growth plates in their bones. She's helping save Pequitos everywhere from having to live and die at the hands of some mean girls who kick it in a clique.

KiKi and me looking "fancy" on my eighteenth birthday. We didn't get into the bar behind us.

The point is, friends are great, but cliques for the sake of clicking your paws on the countertops of someone else's right to enjoy life are nasty, karmically dangerous, and bad if you plan on being in the business of getting anything done in your life shy of lying on your back and counting ceiling tiles. A lot of things in life are horribly tempting, living in Europe for more than a month, giving it up on the first date, lying in the sun covered in Wesson oil, but in the end they are all a bad idea. If you have a righteous group of friends then be righteous and be thankful for one another because a good set of friends can last you a lifetime. Just don't be self-righteous. I know there are Pequitos near you with big bull's-eyes attached to their backs, but next time you feel like piercing one of them with a venomous arrow in front of your friends just imagine how it feels to be on the other end of that poison tip. *It sucks!* Clique wisely, kitten!

Shower Power

Martha Quinn wanted clear skin and a career in rock and roll, I wanted to shave my legs, get a bra, and use deodorant. I wanted to feel womanly, to use mature trinkets and creams. I wanted to have enough hormones to generate malodorous perspiration, acne, excess body hair, and expanded fat cells. Who says young people don't have their priorities straight? I never asked for a public shower, I did just fine on my own with a bar of Ivory and ten minutes of humid solitude. When did I ever demand a public hose-down during the embarrassing start of an awkward and slow-moving puberty? In sixth grade we still had recess and looked forward to footy pajama slumber parties complete with Barbie swapping. Come seventh grade there was a huge shift in priorities, to liquid eyeliner, tongue kissing, maxi pads. How did everything change so drastically in a year? And more important, why did they make us shower in front of everyone after gym class?

There seems to be an unwritten sadistic law among physical education teachers that short shorts and cellulite go hand in hand for instructors and public humiliation of blossoming young women will somehow make them better citizens. The only girls comfortable enough to strut naked in junior high were the ones who had prematurely developed the bodies of twenty-eight-year-old exotic dancers, and we all know how they end up after adolescence (cluck). Quite a few of my counterparts and I did not receive the gift basket from the boob fairy until the end of high school. We would have needed to wear some sort of pubic toupee to fit in with the comfortable set (in Scotland I believe it's called a "mirkin"). Needless to say the days of huddling in the showers were so frustrating. Everyone was giddy for gossip about each other and the deadliest kind was a morsel about someone's physical flaws . . . "Did you hear Mary shaves her back?" . . . "Rene has four nipples and a rash on her thighs." Ooooohh, yuck. That ugliness breeds itself somehow. Don't give in to the dark side.

It's easier to laugh now about the uneasiness of my first days of semipublic nakedness. I didn't get comfortable with my naked body in public (female public) until four or five years ago when I started juggling beer cans with my bare chest at nude beaches outside Sausalito. No, that's not true, they weren't beer cans. Actually I started swimming at a club that seemed to attract unusually obese women as its main clientele. I had no problem changing in front of women who were carrying one hundred to two hundred pounds more than me. Let's face it, one of the great discomforts of nakedness is revealing your flaws and we're all told that there are no flaws more fatal than excessive ridges and bumps of everyday womanhood. Along with that precious leg hair and BO the marked physiological differences in newly arrived womanhood include cellulite and hips. In some respects it is getting a lot better and some bigger women are refusing to change themselves for the camera. Still, I think there is much more praise for looking like

Cameron Diaz than Ricki Lake. I don't hear too many stories about girls struggling to gain weight to fit into that size 14 prom dress so they can look just like Delta Burke in the last season of *Designing Women*. It's just not as common to hear a girl in her teens getting kudos for adding on that extra five pounds the way people coo over a baby that doubles its birth weight in a month.

Whether it's too much or too little the time you are going through right now is filled with enormous self-criticism and doubt. No matter how you look at yourself you don't measure up to who you want to be, what you think your potential is. That's because you aren't there yet, ding-dong! You are literally metamorphosing and girls never give themselves any slack for the time it takes to go from caterpillar to chrysalis to butterfly. Give yourself a rest. No one ever successfully willed themselves to develop more quickly.

I remember going into my mom's room and saying, "Mom, Jill already has a bra and she's only a year older than me. Am I going to need a bra next year? When will my boobies grow?" OK, I don't think I said "boobies," but it's a funny word so I wrote it. A lot of girls were super-flat-chested and the next year their chests shot out of their shirts like tulips in springtime. If you're still waiting for a growth spurt, don't worry, you'll change and then you'll hate the way your new body looks. You can't control the rate at which your body grows so focus on the more important things that you can control.

As far as showering goes, you can do a few things. When other girls criticize you for how you look in the buff just look them up and down, pick out a flaw, and **start giggling at the meanies.** Soap yourself up again and go another round in the hot water. It's important to appear comfortable when you are being attacked. If someone is criticizing you

175

chances are they are terrified of being found out so find their flaw and start needling. If you have unsightly flaps and folds, you could always have a highly skilled and overpaid tattoo artist **tattoo beautiful scenery on your flesh** such as Hawaiian flowers, breathtaking mammals such as lemurs and moose, dragons, or a crying Jesus. That'll distract 'em! But I wouldn't advise it. If your skin starts to shrink with weight loss or expand with muscle gain you could have a plumeria that resembles a birthmark or a goose that looks like a salty earthworm. You could also try **hanging out with women of various body types** such as those who frequent public swimming pools, ocean and river beaches, or parades. You can try **imagining you are somewhere else** instead of a crowded locker room with your bits hanging out. Pretend you are really in a secluded meadow all alone with birds chirping sweet nature songs in your ear as your pet ferret Ross eats the sweet meat of wild mangoes. Ahhh, who cares about a bare fanny when your ferret is happy. You know there are others who feel as miserable and shamed as you do for having a genetic makeup they are unable to control. Find these people and **align yourself with like-minded freaks,** laugh heartily as you make fun of yourselves in all your goofy splendor. No one is perfect, not even a thirteen-year-old with a thirty-eight-inch bust. If it is truly uncomfortable and the teacher is getting some sort of perverse joy out of your pain you can always **create a petition** to have your parents' tax money go toward something worthwhile like shower curtains instead of those pesky books and computers. C'mon, what's more important, forging bonds and sharing ideas with students from other lands over the Internet or protecting your nakedness from your classmates? A lady has to have her priorities.

mONo. Eek! MoNo.

How much can this glandular demon suck? Oh, plenty! Mononucleosis can set a high schooler back months and cause anxiety, depression, and very, very swollen glands. Mono is a virus that you catch when you are swapping fluids by sharing beverages or by smacking chops with Romeo in the backyard. You will know you have mono when your life force has left you and you don't even have the energy to wave it bye-bye.

I got "the kissing disease" when I was a junior. Things were going fabulously (for once). I was in a groovy choir where we got to sing Elvis songs, I had a tan, and this knob Angela had graduated the spring before and couldn't torture me (we called her Elvis because she had really long sideburns). I had been feeling a little puffy, my throat hurt, and my heart was going pitter-pat in an annoying sort of way, the kind of way that makes you feel like you are listening to Paula Abdul records (which can cause symptoms all its own). The doctor was explaining my premature ventricular contractions and was about to tell me why my tum hurt when someone handed him the lab report, which

 177

turned out to be a fate worse than Tori Spelling's nose job. I had the virus! I had the plague! The worst part was I didn't even get it from kissing; I got it from chewing gum out of someone else's mouth (come to think of it, I deserved mono). When you have mono you can't enjoy your much deserved vacation from school because you are far too busy sleeping and damning the heavens because your glands are so swollen and your throat is so sore you can't even talk on the phone, not that there is anyone to talk to because anyone not in school is a loser or far too old for you. The first few days might be really kosher, you ease into sleeping late and watching Sally Jesse , you nibble on some sherbet and maybe field one or two phone calls from concerned friends calling to check in. Then the African sleeping sickness part of it sets in and you can't even stand up without listening to a five-part Anthony Robbins motivational tape. Your body starts to go downhill and then morale declines, because—remember those phone calls?—your friends have all forgotten about you because they have the attention spans of Chihuahuas on cappuccino and have filled your place at the lunch table with their vinyl knapsacks. Your eyes hurt too bad to watch TV so you lie around with a washcloth on your face reliving the glory days of algebra exams and *Ethan Frome* pop quizzes in your head.

There are a few items that can get you through the dark days. Here is a list of four things that will somehow get you through that dark tunnel of spit-born illness, and eventually show you the light at the end. **L-lysine.** In our world of vitamins, herbs, and supplements this is an age-old amino acid that reduces swollen glands and lessens the effects of the virus. It also works well for cold sores and general sore throats. **Catch up.** Undoubtedly your teachers will expect some homework from you, and since you will be sore, tired, and partially incapacitated, you may as well "read" one or two of the assigned classics by checking out some books on tape from the library. **Do some thinkin'.** This time alone is a fabulous occasion to reflect and rethink some of the important tasks that need doing but never get done. Decide on the color you want to repaint your room, think of creative ways to extort money for a new car or a trip to the birthplace of American Sweetheart and your idol Tonya Harding. You may not be able to act, but you still have your dreams. **Rest.** Your body is obviously run-down, and did you know you can burst a swollen spleen with too much physical activity during a bout with mono? Don't chance it. Sleep and sleep and sleep some more, and before you know it you will be back in ceramics class craving a good nap and a prechewed piece of gum.

Oh, and strike that last thing . . . *don't* chew gum out of other people's mouths. It's very unladylike.

Mono. Eek! Mono.

Smoke This, sHEbA

Your teeth  are so young and healthy and bright! Why would you want to jeopardize the most accessible lovely part of your face? I hate smoking, 🚬 I think I am allergic. I think smoking is particularly unpleasant for younger women because it deceives them into thinking they actually look cool, while all the while they are building up icky carcinogens in their bloodstream, lungs, and on their once white fingertips. I am not trying to sound like a goody-goody telling you that you can't smoke. Of course you can! You are a woman of your own will and hopefully your intuition is telling you that cigarette smoke is stinky and steals the very life from your tender pink lungs.

I can relate. My affair with Count Nicotine started at a disastrously young age, eleven, and took a brief leave of absence when I was fifteen. You know why? Do you know what the pleasures of riding the camel gave me? Strep throat. My throat was so irritated from it and bacteria was buried so deep within my tonsils that no amount of antibiotics could come close to cleansing them. Nice Dr. Coale ripped them from me, my poor bloody tonsils! Don't worry, they are dried up in a paper bag under my old bed at my mom's. She thinks I threw them away when I moved to California. Shhhhh. Smoking also increased my heart rate, which was very convenient since I already had a minor heart condition.

I did quit for two years, but I started again at seventeen when all my friends and I went to Hawaii for our high school graduation. I remember where I was when the dragon reentered my lungs. It was a cheesy diner in Waikiki a few blocks down the street from our hotel

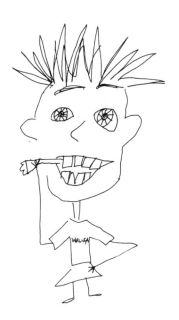 where you could watch the Rottweiler-size cockroaches battle nightly. I smoked and I smoked and I chatted about life while the life in my own lungs faded with every exhalation of the burning, chemical-soaked tobacco leaves. I did this a few times every day for the next two years and I coughed and wheezed without a care. I would switch to menthols sometimes (goes down much easier with bronchitis and green mucus). When I was working at KROQ on the overnight shift and the station was dark and empty and the phones were dead, I would light up and play smoke ring games and pretend I was Ava Gardner (she was such a glamorous smoker, and married to Frank Sinatra,

ya know) until the sun came up and it was finally time to go. Do you know what finally made me quit the yuck mouth habit for good? Mountain biking. I had taken to the sport because I was so susceptible to illness (especially upper respiratory infections) and was tired of feeling weak all the time. For a while I blamed it on the pollution. Each day after work I'd pull out my bike and head into the Hollywood Hills up the fire roads and past the coyotes, until my lungs just wouldn't let me pedal anymore. One day I made an important connection. I realized that the fewer cigarettes I smoked, the greater my lung capacity, and the greater my lung capacity the farther I rode, and the farther I rode the better I slept and the better I slept the better my skin looked . . . and so on and so forth until one day I had quit smoking altogether, and that may be one of the nicest things I have ever done for myself. Although I still get bronchitis which sucks because I fly a lot and we all know planes are breeding grounds for talkative morons and airborne germs. I also like to take in the rock and roll music shows, but that is a little more difficult because everyone who is trying to enjoy nice rock smokes about six packs 🚬 a night and that leads to some pretty irritated lovely parts, dry, itchy eyes, and an occasional bloody nose. The bloody nose is usually from a nasty fistfight, but we'll leave that out for now.

What the hell am I talking all this do-gooder no smoking nonsense for? I am trying to deprive you of the wonders of yellow teeth and fingers that will turn gray by the time you're thirty. Then people will *really* know you are a chic and sensible force to be reckoned with because you are a smoker and that makes you cool and rebellious and French. Did I mention horse's ass ashtray mouth? By gum if you decide to smoke you are in for an activity teeming with femininity and social grace. You will be so attractive you won't even need a boyfriend. Who needs all that baggage? Who needs friends when you'll be dying too soon or you'll be too sick to have fun with them anyway?

Smoke This, Sheba

rAIny dAY Lady

Another thing I wish I had done growing up is save more money. My friend LuLu had a dad with a nickel fetish who filled up a water jug every chance he got with his loose pocket change. I wonder if he walked around their house jingling it in his pocket just to tease her. At the end of the day he would trickle the silver (who needs pennies? I think they should be abolished, they take up too much space) into her magic jug for a rainy day. I'm not sure if they were expecting her to need the clanky dough for a new kidney, but they didn't let her near the loot until she was old enough to vote and enter the military. When she was eighteen she only wanted to buy handbags and Asian stocks and those are two things she found very difficult to purchase with pocket change. Have you ever tried to unload a purse full of dimes at Barney's New York? By the time young LuLu came of age and began looking to leave her parents' nest interest rates were very attractive and she decided she would rather purchase an apartment than blow ten years' worth of rent. It was a very wise and commendable decision, and if you have the same means in a milk jug I suggest you do the

185

Me and my dad after a patriotic concert at Lakeridge High. He still thinks I'm in law school.

same. It would not have been possible, the down payment would have been far from her grasp, were it not for the nonchalant generosity of her father and the spare silver he saved for a good twenty years. She had close to ten thousand dollars 💰 in her jug! She could have easily been foolish and gotten a pair of fake jugs in her chest, but she chose to invest in her housing future.

I wish I had gotten into the habit of saving money from the odd jobs I worked in high school. When I was a lot younger my mom would give me incentive to weed the yard and clean my messy room by greasing me with a one-dollar bill now and again. Sometimes she would just make a credit sheet for me and write down the dollars earned here and there, and when I had done enough menial labor she walked me to the savings and loan (thanks to Chuck Keating we don't got those no more) and opened a savings account with fifty smackaroonies. My lazy brothers were so jealous! Here I was at eight years old with my own lavish savings account. By the time I turned ten I had a chocolate addiction that reached massive desperation. Needless to say, or maybe it requires thorough explanation, I sponged off my own savings account to buy peanut butter cups and gob stoppers until I was flat broke in less than a year. My shoe fetish knew no bounds after that, so every penny I earned in adolescence went to loafers and platforms. I didn't pick up

186

Kennedy

the saving bug until I was well into my twenty-third year. That's when the regrets came rushing in, that's when I knew I had blown millions in lost IRA money and tax shelters. Why didn't I save? Why why why? I coulda had an apartment at sixteen, I could be driving a new Jag to school instead of riding in KiKi's Sprint, I could have saved for a second home in Alabama. Well, you can't go cleaning the kitchen sink forever, but if you can get the work and make the loot, take it. When you get the desire for independence nothing spells freedom like cash, and in order to get it you need to take a few responsible steps.

Money: It helps to have steady income, whether it's baby-sitting, making and selling clothes, cold-calling for insurance agents, being a receptionist, retail on the weekends . . . etc. A lot of adults think that having a job while you're still in school diminishes your homework time and creates desperation. This may be true, so see if your parents will put you on an allowance or let you sell your plasma once a month. Others think having steady work encourages good habits like punctuality, good social skills, and overall responsibility, not to mention providing a steady income which allows for even more responsibility.

The Habit: Once you start saving consistently you really develop an addiction to it, especially if you can tap into it for an emergency or a really special occasion. Seeing your cash grow is very comforting because you finally have a sense of financial security and personal pride. Money is by no means the only way of achieving this, but I feel it's very important for women to be financially capable always. It's a lot easier to maintain habits that start early.

187

Consistency: Try and save the same amount in a given time, whether it's fifty dollars a month or four dollars a year. When you save it really does become a habit and you start to do it automatically. Even when you are hardly making a thing, when you deduct that little bit it will grow like a wild Chia pet in no time.

Pay to the Order of: You! You should be the first person who gets paid whenever you receive a paycheck or allowance. You will always have to take care of yourself and it's easier to extract money from your savings account than to try to take back your Prada bag when you need cash to visit Grandma after her operation. There will always be time to buy stuff. Just remember to skim a little for your stash each time the green touches your hand. Grandma will thank you!

Incentive: Set saving goals for yourself. Maybe it's a thousand dollars in a year, or one hundred dollars, whatever. Once you reach that goal have something in mind for yourself and go get it, just don't blow your entire nest egg. The nicer you are to yourself in the present by saving money and starting good habits the longer the dividends will pay off and you will feel a lot better about yourself because no one will have to support you once you get on your own two feet. As I said, the younger you start doing it the faster your diligence will pay off.

Whether your parents are saving change in a canister or you baby-sit for your cousins twice a month, taking care of yourself by saving even a little money will always pay off. It will be one of those things you can thank yourself for and one more thing your parents can get off your back about. It is always incredibly attractive to a boy to see a bright young thing with her own savings account who is building good credit. It spells independence, and there is nothing more attractive to a young buck. Don't let him freeload off you . . . even if he is the cutest, sweetest trombonist in the world don't go out of your way to blow your wad on a boy. They are never worth depleting your hard-earned money. Happy saving!

SaVInG WiTh Fran

Fran Seegull is an excellent example of a rainy day lady who put her umbrella and mind to good use. As a graduate of Harvard Business School (an MBA from HBS is considered "the most powerful degree in the world") Fran devotes her time and energy to helping revive the self-esteem of young women everywhere by teaching financial independence and business know-how. She is creative, assertive, and a management consultant for the entertainment division of Price Waterhouse.

All right, Fran, why is saving important? I think that saving is incredibly important because it is kind of a precursor to economic independence. By that I mean that you are moving toward a place where you are working, and you'll be saving and you will no longer be reliant upon your parents or your grandparents or anybody else for that matter; to be fully independent, economically independent, socially independent in every way. I think that saving is particularly important for girls be-

191

cause traditionally girls have not saved and it's been very much where the man, either your boyfriend or your husband, would take care of you. We're thankfully in a time right now in this country where women are moving to a point where there is more economic parity with men. There is still a wage gap, but it is closing and women have so many

opportunities professionally. Making your own way, saving your own money, and providing for yourself are linked, I believe, to self-esteem, to financial independence, and to, really, emotional independence. You are in a situation where if you are out on a date you can pay for your half. And that is a kind of empowerment where you don't owe anything to the guy at the end of the evening because he paid. I think that saving is really very critical for girls. **Why is it more exciting to shop than to save?** It is definitely more tempting to shop than it is to save. The distinction is between instant gratification and delayed gratification. If you are out in a mall and you buy the bottle of Hard Candy nail polish that is pretty much instant gratification, you can go home and put it on and it is very immediate. To me saving is about delayed gratification and it is almost a higher-order type of activity where you are saving for the future. You're saving because you feel it is important to provide for yourself. I think at the end of the day it has to be a very healthy mix between instant gratification, that is going out and buying the nail polish or buying the CD, and delayed gratification, which could take the form of saving to buy something for yourself that is bigger later. **Why is it good to start saving at an early age?** This is something we talked a lot about at business school. It is called the Time Value of Money. What that means is that a dollar today can be worth more tomorrow. If you earn a 10 percent interest on a dollar per year, your dollar today will be worth $1.10 tomorrow. Then you get interest on the interest, which is called compound interest. This means in the first year you have a dollar, at the end of the first year you have $1.10, at the end of the second year you will have $1.21; you are earning interest on your interest. That's a very powerful tool through which to increase your savings. So if you can sock away just a little bit every month or every week, you will be surprised at how much you will have at the end of the year, and if you invest it wisely, in a place that will give you interest on your deposits, you will have a really wonderful nest egg in not too long a time. **Does saving make you more attractive?** Well, I definitely think it does. This takes us back to the issue we were talking about earlier, which is the connection between girls' self-esteem and money. We know that money is part of what makes the world go around and money enables self-sufficiency, and I think that can be quite empowering for women and girls. **Let's say you earned enough money and wanted to start a business. How would you go about doing that?** You need to start with a skill, a skill that you can convert into a product. It can be a service like baby-sitting or it can be a product like silk-screened T-shirts. The most important thing, in the T-shirt example, is to maybe make a small set of prototypes. Now, marketing is absolutely a key piece. That could be putting up flyers at school, it could be wearing the T-shirts at school and peo-

193

ple remarking on them and putting orders in. The most financially savvy way to do it is to make your T-shirts to order. So someone likes a particular one, or say you have six and you can invite a small group of friends over to your house, show [the shirts] to them and then make [shirts] in the sizes and colors they want. If you can make a product that is very specific to someone, like a size or a color that they really like, perhaps you can charge more. And then you have to start keeping books and again the Sources and Uses statements are really important. Find out how much the revenue line is going to be. Like if I sell ten T-shirts at ten dollars each per month I am going to make one hundred dollars a month. Then find out how much the T-shirts themselves cost, that is called the Cost of Goods Sold. Figure out how much the T-shirts and the labor (you are probably going to want to pay yourself in the equation) are going to cost, and then you can start figuring out how many T-shirts you need to make and sell in order to make it worthwhile. There are many ways to start a business and that is just one simple example of a home-based business that doesn't require too much capital up front. **Tell me about the camp you are involved in.** I am a camp counselor at a camp called Camp Start-up. There is one in northern California and one at Wellesley, which is the one I am going to be at. The goal of the camp is to teach girls economic independence. We do this through a very special series of lesson plans, and the types of skills that we try to teach are pretty broad. They are basic business skills, the concept of entrepreneurship, and this gets back to your question of how do I start a business and teaches girls to start a business and start thinking about all the ingredients that go into making a business. We also teach girls about leadership, giving back to your community, self-esteem issues, how to work in teams, role models, and

194

the importance of mentors in their lives. It promises to be a really interesting experience. There are thirty girls that come ages thirteen to eighteen and there are five counselors and we basically write business plans together. A business plan is basically a blueprint for a business that could be built after the camp if someone were so inclined. **That sounds amazing, Fran. Good luck!**

Hello, Kitty!

Have you ever sat around bored to tears wondering what it would be like to be more feline-esque? Have you thought, "Wow . . . cats really have it made!" Research has shown that about eight out of ten Americans feel just that way—being catlike is very attractive. Seventy-nine percent of Americans polled say they would like to have one or more cat characteristics, 58 percent admitted to owning one or more cats, 43 percent preferred cats to dogs, 71 percent would never consider owning a ferret, 13 percent said they had seen the Andrew Lloyd Webber musical *Cats,* and 12 percent said they had been bitten by cats. How nice would it be to lie around and stretch six or seven times an hour, to stare mysteriously at someone until they rub your jowls, to poop in boxes, to nap . . . weeeeell, maybe not poop in boxes. As a people we can agree on one thing—we all love to nap! That's it, 110 percent of us have been bitten by catnap fever! I'm not talking about the litter box bacterium that rests undetectably in cat claws causing encephalitis and coma if you are susceptible and get scratched by one of the furry devils—that's cat-*scratch* fever. I'm talking about a nationwide craving for naps! When I worked as an accountant in Barcelona for twenty years we would shut the office down after a big lunch of Spanish fritters and custard and all go into a big air-conditioned room in the summer (Barcelona gets *very* hot), lie down on

our cots, and nap for forty-five minutes. The first month it was very hard for me to nap with the whole extradition mess hanging over my head, but I easily settled into the habit when they threatened to fire me—I was disturbing people with my incessant knuckle cracking and distracting whimpering. When the time came for me to leave Spain and head back to trial in the United States I sure didn't miss my assumed identity or the tamale pie, but I did miss those afternoons curled up in a ball where my jaw relaxed and my head floated away in total bliss. The post-luncheon clearheadedness actually made me more productive. I was able to fudge five or six more books a day than before, I was on the phone threatening more people than ever to pay their gambling debts. Was this phenomenon unique to me?

As it turns out, no it was not. Scientists have tirelessly studied the effects of adherence to a rigorous napping schedule, and for the curious and willing the results are good. In addition to increased concentration and enhanced performance napping also provides relaxation, a time for the brain to shut down in the middle of the day when stress is high and hormones are going crazy. Sleep is when your bones and hair grow and it rejuvenates the cells, especially in the skin. That's why so many people experience what is known in the industry as "nap-per's glow." Ritual nappers are healthier, happier, better-looking, calm and relaxed . . . an all-around joy to be around. Forget the stuff the military teaches you about teamwork and responsibility, *I* don't want a zinged-out jar-head barking orders at me, I want someone who naps! I want to hire the lady who has enough discipline and character to lie down each day, to admit when she's tired, someone who will take charge of her own life.

I don't think I am alone in this. I am convinced there are more people like me who need a nap. I made some calls to my friends and family to see what *they* thought about napping. Here's how it went. First I called my sister-in-law Dana. She is a mom with a toddler and a newborn, so I figured she herself would be tired and probably seemed like a good person to ask about napping. She said a solid nap gives her a clear head and allows her to do more things in a day that she wouldn't be able to do without twenty minutes or so of kitty sleep. My friend Chris is a hard-working contractor with a tool belt and a mean schedule who rarely has time to eat a Taco Bell Grande, let alone budget time each day to steal for his sleep deficit. He is only 5´1˝ tall and he is convinced he would have grown to be a lot taller if he had gotten the required eight hours of sleep a night in addition to a one-hour power snooze necessary for growing adolescents. His 6´11˝ father was in the NBA. My friend Lucinda, who likes smelly candles and Winnie the Pooh, brought it home best when she said, "Naps are good, they are like milk." Now, ladies, she may not be an expert, but here is a smart lady who knows a few good cat qualities when she sees them. Milk? Naps? Next thing I know she'll be giving herself a tongue bath and preening with her butt in the air; we should all strive for such balance.

Hello, Kitty!

As you can clearly see, a lot of people are in search of the key to longer, happier lives and they are happy to find an oasis in the desert of this thing we call living. There is no more stressful gymnasium a human can find than in the confines of a high school or junior high. Hormones are firing like homies in the LBC, teachers and parents are unrealistic and demanding, and peers are unrelenting and venomous. To put it lightly, it's not very catlike. Next time you get home from school why add salt to the wound by immediately diving into that homework? Why not lay your head down, let your thoughts float where they may, and give in to a healthy, purr-worthy nap? Would Felix and I steer you wrong?

Kennedy

Monica

They asked me to be the spokesperson for BBC, Boarding for Breast Cancer, a snowboarding event designed to raise money for breast cancer research, and I could never say no. My friends put it on, I was honored by the invitation, and my mother is a survivor of breast cancer. That was a particularly devastating time in my life, finding out my mom was sick, watching her go through chemotherapy, admiring this brave woman for holding barbecues every single weekend I was home and not eating a thing because the sores in her mouth and throat were way too painful to chew or swallow. It wasn't too painful to laugh and it certainly wasn't too painful to give me words of strength and encouragement during a summer when I was sure I was going to fall apart. When I hear a beautiful, inspiring story of a woman struggling with breast cancer I usually cry. I picture my mom and her cute bald head painting angels at her desk. A doctor angel for her oncologist, two tennis-playing angels with red Afros for the Jensen brothers. Each day a new angel, a new reason to get out of bed and put on makeup, a new way to play with my niece because she had gotten too heavy for my mom to lift, a new way to inspire me. I was reduced to a girl again that summer, begging desperately each day not to have my mommy taken away. Luckily she's still here and she inspires me just about every day. She looked really great bald. Before cancer her hair was stick-straight, beautiful black shiny hair. All she ever wanted was a perm! They never took, and with all those chemicals having entered and left her body she'll never put too many more near her if she can help it. In November of that year, right before the holidays, the funniest thing happened. My mom turned into a poodle! Her hair is now the thickest, curliest, blackest poodle hair you could ever imagine, and she didn't have to blow the eighty bucks on a perm. That is inspiring. She is an angel.

As I was getting ready for my duties at BBC, the organizers were kind enough to give me some articles about the previous two BBC's so I knew what the event was about and who inspired it. It wasn't just a day to ride around with friends in the sun, listening to bands and watching pros ride. There was the neatest story written by a girl named Monica who was battling breast cancer. She had a double mastectomy and was on her second round of chemotherapy. Her body was tired and her family was frightened, but she was finding there were indeed ways of coping with the great unknown. Her arms were so sore from surgery, because she had her underarm lymph nodes removed. She compared the pain of not knowing if you were going to live or die with being sucked into a black hole. It's so easy to get pulled in and give in to the hopelessness of the seemingly inevitable darkness of death. Instead Monica decided to fight. She wanted to find ways to remain in the sun. She wanted to experience everything she possibly could and feel each day like it was her first and live it like it was her last. Every day as she woke and got out of bed she put her feet on the ground and realized how incredible it is to have feet at all. She could have dwelt on the pain of being so young and having that cancer inside eating her body and her bones. Instead she marveled at the idea of feet and the people who aren't fortunate enough to be able to use them. She'd stretch her swollen arms up to the sky and giggle with wonder at how nice it is to stretch and touch. She forgot when she was well to be thankful for everything beautiful in her life, and at this point, because she chose to see it that way, every single thing she came in contact with was beautiful. Things she never chose to see before, experiences and people she took for granted, they were all there before her to love. In the article she begged everyone to look around them and take note of the things in our lives we take for granted, the things we neglect. She asked that the next time we wake up we put our feet on the ground and look around and appreciate at least one thing each day that we would normally pass by. Nothing is worth neglecting.

Monica passed away in February of 1996. Because her cancer was detected too late it got the better of her young body and took her from her family, her husband, her friends, and the beautiful mountains she loved to carve around on her snowboard. Her body may have given way but in her heart she lived each remaining day she had, she fought for her spirit, and in that way she lives on. When I read her story I was so inspired. My face was wet from crying, not just because it makes me so sad to hear about another woman going through this ordeal while her family ached, but also because in dying she lived as we all should— free from the useless negativity and destructive thoughts that kill people faster than any cancer. When I wake up in a bad mood, or I'm pissed off because some dumbass just cut me off in line at the store, or whatever brings me down in a day, I try to think of Monica. Her words uplift me and ultimately make me a little lighter. That is inspiring. She was an angel.

Pay Attention

Pay attention. This time in your life happens so fast and vividly and it's bound to be over soon enough. You will look back at being young in one of two ways. You may have hated it in which case you will enjoy your adult life a lot more. If this is so and you are hating youth then pay attention to how it feels because when you are successful later you will look back at what hell you went through and will feel somewhat justified. If you are loving being young, which is a wonderful way to live, then you will always recall these years with immense fondness and will practically kill yourself in order to recapture some of the purity. No matter what you do in life, whether it's drinking from a fountain at 2:37 P.M. on August 24 or ringing in a new millennium, just be cognizant of the fact that this moment, whatever moment you are in, will never, ever happen again. Things may be similar but they'll never be the same. Life may get better and better for you but your senses will be dulled to each new experience of beauty because everything is only new once. Pay attention to how it feels to be sad and desperate and lonely and betrayed. At some point you may be hardened from these

Me at age three with Santa and my brothers Allen and Brian.

things to a degree, so remember how they feel. That way when the sun ☼ shines for you again you can appreciate warmth and the moment will be whole. You will be held accountable for so much more as you get older, personally and as a part of society, so relish the carefree days when you sleep late and laugh out loud. Always pay attention to where you are and anticipate what you're getting into so you're prepared to deal with whatever comes. Weigh your options and laugh at yourself when it's all over. Every new obstacle and heartache will never be new again, so you won't be surprised when they happen the second time around. Just as every bug 🐛 and flower ✿ are magical to a baby, take in all the positive things you see so later on you can remember what it was like to be young and pure and to have felt it all. Pay attention.

Kennedy

Acknowledgments

I have a lot of people to thank so bear with me. My mom and dad, the two hardest-working, smartest people I know. My brothers Brian and Allen for the guidance and humor. The rest of my family, especially Mima and Grandma for their love and baked goods. All my favorite teachers—Mr. and Mrs. Bartman, Miss Popick, Ms. Macomber, Mr. Bullard, Mr. Jordan, Ms. Montague, Madame Streeter, Mr. Swaggard, Hurd, Hutch, Jack, Mr. Ticen, Sahni, and most of all that magical Mr. Wendt, by far the most inspiring teacher one could ever hope to have. Thanks to all my friends at MTV—Andy, Sheri, Cindy, Lauren and Lauren, Laslo, Carolee, Jimmy, Audrey, Kurt, Jenny and Ray, Tabitha, Simon, Idalis, John Norris, John Sencio, Healy, Gil, Lew, Adam, Katty, Powers, Summer, George, Bloom, Juliette, Fab, JenPal, Tina, Gena, Beth, all the wonderful people in the studio, Evans, Austin, Chrissy and Deb, Brian, Doug, Judy, and Tom. I know I forgot people but I'm sorry because I'm a little rushed right now. My KROQ party people—

Jed, Bean, Tami, Kevin, Sluggo, John Frost, Tohru, Scott, Emily, Trip and Kevin, Annoying Scott, Raymondo, Lisa, Rick, and Anne. Special thanks to Adam and Drew, everyone at Conan, Bill and everyone at PI, and the amazing Maria and Howard and the whole Lapides Entertainment family, especially Chip. Thanks to my incredible literary agent Tina Bennett and every devoted soul at Janklow Nesbit especially Mort Janklow. Thanks to past agents and friends Doug Robinson, Jeff and Stephanie Jacobs, Ted Miller, Bruce Vinokour, and Michael Camacho. Thank you, Joel Lipsky! My trusty proofreaders Michele, Geraldine, Pete, Uncle Millsey, Johnny, Jess, Megan, Glen, Barrett, Temple, Andrea and Chris, Dweezil, and my fantasmastical stepdad Bob. He's Irish. Official thanks to the women of the WNBA—Stacey, Alice, Terry, and especially Jamila. Thanks to Dr. Gendler for squeezing me in, Father Al for his guidance and arrangements with the sisters, Fran and her nice aunt and uncle, Mrs. Haynes for her insight, Tina B, and Sandra. Special love to Guy-O, Caresse, and Madonna (why not?), Suzanne Smith, Rick Gentile, Matt Maranz. The beautiful families that helped me along the way the Hoefers, the Zappas, the entire Arentine Circus, the Froelichs, the Bittners, the Lees, the Schepmans, the D'Arcangelos. Thank you Denell Downum, my magnificent editor, and all the people at Doubleday, including Bruce Tracy, Pat Mulcahy, and artsy Jean. Janel for her remarkable transcription, Jaime at Kinko's. I love all my ladies . . . Dana, Quentin, Audrey, Isabella, Pud, Sherida, Elena, Kelly, Carrie, Paige K, Paige W, Kristen, Marsha, Sharon, Dana C, Hanna, Ingrid, and Andree.

Most of all I want to thank my DL. I love you Dave!